VICTORIAN BRAY
A town adapts to changing times

Maynooth Studies in Local History

GENERAL EDITOR Raymond Gillespie

This is one of six new pamphlets published in 1998 in the Maynooth Studies in Local History series. Like their fourteen predecessors these volumes illustrate, through case studies of particular areas and themes, how life in Ireland in the past evolved in a variety of settings, both urban and rural. As such they join a rapidly growing literature dealing with the local dimension of Ireland's past. That 'localness' is not primarily territorial, although all are firmly rooted in a sense of place, but derives from an awareness of the regional diversity of Irish society in the past.

Local history is not about administrative frameworks or geographical entities but rather about the people who created the social worlds which made particular places distinctive. These pamphlets are therefore primarily about people who lived in particular places over time. The range of people explored is wide; from the poor of pre-famine Drogheda and Ferbane through the nouveau riche world of the Meath grazier to the aristocratic lifestyle of an eighteenth-century Tipperary landlord. What all these people have in common is that they shaped their particular places in response to stimuli both from within their communities and from the wider world.

Like their predecessors these pamphlets allow us a brief glimpse into the diverse, interacting worlds which are the basis of the Irish historical experience. In their own right they are each significant contributions to our understanding of that experience in all its richness and complexity. They present local history as the vibrant and challenging discipline that it is.

Maynooth Studies in Local History: Number 18

Victorian Bray

A Town Adapts to Changing Times

Liam Clare

IRISH ACADEMIC PRESS

First published in 1998 by
IRISH ACADEMIC PRESS
44, Northumberland Road, Dublin 4, Ireland
and in North America by
IRISH ACADEMIC PRESS
c/o ISBS, 5804 NE Hassalo Street, Portland, OR 97213
website: http://www.iap.ie

British Library Cataloguing in Publication Data

Clare, Liam
  Victorian Bray: an administrative perspective. – (Maynooth
  studies in local history)
  1. Local government – Ireland – Bray – History – 19th
  century 2. Bray (Ireland) – Politics and government 3. Bray
  (Ireland) – History – 19th century
  I. Title 351.4'1838

  ISBN 0–7165–2700–6

Typeset in 10 pt on 12 pt Bembo by
Carrigboy Typesetting Services, County Cork
Printed by ColourBooks Ltd., Dublin

Contents

Acknowledgements

I wish to record my thanks to the many people who gave me encouragement, advice, information and support during my research.

To Dr. Dympna McLoughlin, my thesis supervisor, for her advice, guidance and encouragement; to Dr. Raymond Gillespie, Course Director, and Mary Ann Lyons, Acting Course Director who were both extremely supportive.

To the staffs of the National Library, the National Archives, Maynooth College Library, the Royal Irish Academy Library, Brighton Reference Library, and the Gilbert Library, particularly to Dr. Máire Kennedy, librarian at the Gilbert, for their assistance in my research.

To Mr. Blaise Treacy, Wicklow County Manager, who gave me access to the records of the Bray Town Commissioners and Bray Urban District Council, and to other members of his staff, particularly Pat Downes and Joan Kavanagh in Wicklow Court House, Eileen Murray, Michael Kelleher and Carmel Moore of the County Wicklow library service, and Seamus Ó Dunlaing of Bray Urban District Council.

To the Right Honourable the earl of Meath, Kilruddery, Bray, who provided access to appropriate material in the Meath papers, and took a personal interest in my research, to his secretary Ms Sally-Anne Robertson, and also to Ms. Aideen Ireland of the National Archives, who arranged the contact with Kilruddery.

To Ms. K.M. Davies who facilitated my access to material in the Royal Irish Academy, and to Mary Clark, Dublin City Archivist, and Vincent Moore, Dublin Corporation, for access to waterworks material; to Jacinta Prunty for access to the proofs of her *Dublin Slums 1800–1925*.

To James Scannell, Brian White and Maire and Padraig Laffan for their comments on the text.

To Joan Donnelly who not only typed the script but gave me invaluable editorial advice.

This pamphlet is dedicated to my wife Carmel in acknowledgement of her patience and continued support.

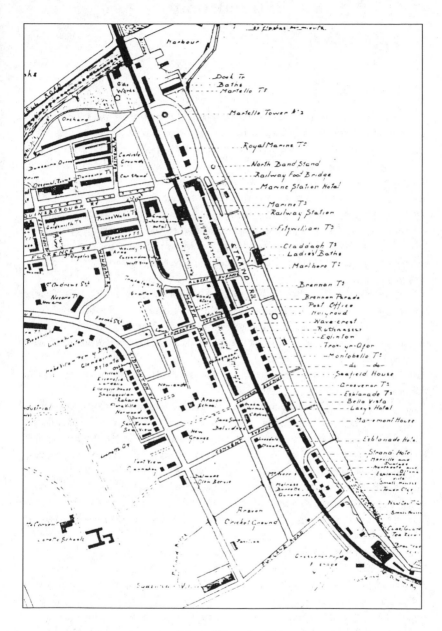

Map 1 Victorian Bray
From A.L. Doran, *Bray and environs* (Bray, 1903)

Introduction

V*ictorian Bray* aims to explore, from an administrative perspective, the pressures and influences on the community in Bray over the period of sixty-four years from 1837. These include the arrival of the railway, the development of the town as a seaside resort, and the rapid population increase, together with national political, social and technological developments, particularly as reflected in legislation and administrative arrangements. Its ancillary objectives are to provide a basis for further studies of the many themes addressed within, to create comparative material for studies of other urban areas or of urban legislation in the centenary year of democratic local government, and to provide background data for the study of other Bray themes with administrative associations.

The period studied, though lengthy, is particularly appropriate, being easily defined, while incorporating administrative growth in Bray from its inception to the arrival of democratic local government in 1899. Constraints of space meant the exclusion of central services, notably police and education, the county administration located in Wicklow town, and the board of guardians based in Loughlinstown. Space also limited development of many of the themes studied.

Traditionally Bray local historians had limited secondary literature to consult. Scott, Doran and Seymour (alias 'an old inhabitant'), used the antiquarian's, the guide-book writer's and the 'reminiscences-of-the-gentry' approach respectively.[1] More recently, Isolde Moylan's thesis in 1972, Arthur Flynn's *History of Bray* (alas no footnotes) in 1986, and the wider scope of *The book of Bray* in 1989, were much more comprehensive in approach.[2] Many articles and studies have also appeared, and much valuable research has been carried out by Bray's two Local Historical Societies. The Royal Irish Academy's *Bray*, in its Irish Historic Towns Atlas series is an added boon. Finally the file of County Wicklow newspaper references on all types of subjects, from 1763 to 1914, by the late Charles J. Coughlan, is uniquely valuable for researchers.[3]

It is the author's hope that this study's broad interpretative approach will make a useful contribution to the historiography of Bray and of local government in Ireland, by extending the frontiers of existing knowledge, by opening up new lines of enquiry, and by stimulating further research.

This study is based on the author's M.A. thesis submitted to the Department of Modern History, National University of Ireland Maynooth, in July 1997.[4]

Bray in 1837 was a small unremarkable town situated around a bridge across the River Dargle. Big Bray or Greater Bray in County Wicklow was sited on a cliff to the south, and consisted of 'the street of Bray', later Main Street. Little Bray in County Dublin, was situated in the floor of the river valley. A small industrial area was tucked in between the cliff and the river. A narrow track led from the town to the sea-shore, where there were two isolated settlements of fishermen's cottages. A small hamlet, Newtown Vevay, existed a mile to the south, and there was ribbon development as far as Old Connaught on the Dublin Road.[5]

The town's location on the main Dublin/Wexford road, some eighteen kilometres south of Dublin, was already attracting wealthier Dubliners. Country residences and summer villas could be bought, leased or rented. Private horse-drawn cars and public omnibuses linked the area with the city.[6] But Bray remained essentially a market town with some industry – brewing and milling, and there was a small sea-borne trade and some fishing. Already Bray was known as 'the gateway to the garden of Ireland' and Quin's hotel, established in 1776, catered for those seeking the scenic pleasures of County Wicklow.[7]

In 1839 Richard Muggeridge, Assistant Poor Law Commissioner, noted a 'greater portion of opulent and intelligent gentry [in Rathdown union] than in any other union in the Kingdom, the metropolis alone excepted' but never-theless pointed out that 'mendicancy in Bray and Kingstown (Dun Laoghaire) [was] almost intolerable'. General Sir George Cockburn, admittedly a colourful maverick, described the poor in Bray and surrounding areas as 'herding like pigs' in overcrowded cabins bereft of furniture, living on oatmeal, potatoes and milk, very badly clothed, but with constant employment of the able-bodied.[8] Crime was rare. Many landlords took a benevolent interest in their tenants, particularly the Putland family, who provided a school for children, a cottage industry for women, and clothing and other necessities for the poor in times of need.[9]

The coming of the railway in 1854 triggered the construction of new terraces and hotels, and facilitated the growth of the town as a seaside resort and a city suburb. Population level expanded rapidly. Many of the new arrivals were upper-class Dubliners, Tory and Protestant, fleeing the decline in their political power and the social decay of the inner city.[10]

This pamphlet explores how the people of Bray responded to the changing milieu: how they interacted with each other; how they coped with evolving concepts of local administration; how they tried to build up the new, tidy up the old, and tackle the town's public health problems.

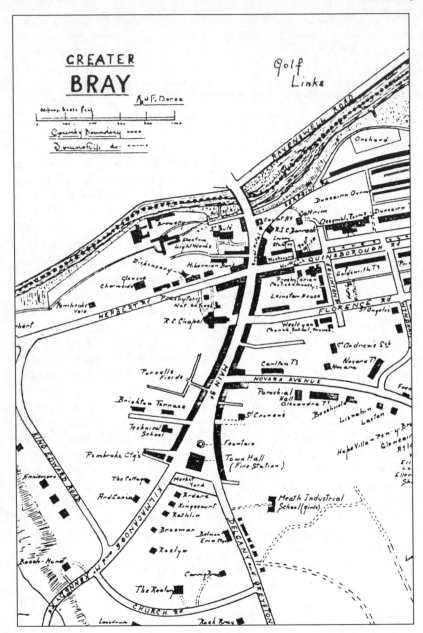

Map 2. Main Street area
From A.L. Doran, *Bray and environs* (Bray, 1903)

The Political Arena

This pamphlet begins by exploring Bray's experience in addressing its emerging needs within an evolving system of local government, an environment in which decisions were made, sometimes harmoniously, sometimes following discordant interaction between civic leaders of opposing views. In 1837, an urban local authority was seen as a medium for providing on a community basis, just a few basic urban services such as public lighting; by 1901 an Urban District Council was a general purpose body with potential interests ranging from abattoirs to zymotic diseases. Other trends also affected local politics, such as the gradual growth of nationalist/Catholic influence (paralleling growth in Catholic property ownership), the imposition of a more democratic electoral system in 1899, and the gradual loss of influence by the earl of Meath, the lord of the manor.

On two occasions in 1840, the lord lieutenant ordered the convening of meetings in Bray for the purpose of adopting the Lighting of Towns Act 1828, and establishing Town Commissioners.[1] Both attempts failed. No contemporary records appear to have survived, but John Quin, hotelier and developer, asserted in 1852 that the 'gentlemen on the periphery of the town' voted unanimously for town commissioners but voted against 'a very small tax' to be imposed.[2] This conflict between spenders and ratepayers is discernible throughout this study and was a major obstacle to municipal development.

The decision to reject Town Commissioners was based on the narrow view that a local authority was merely a provider of services paid for by the ratepayers. It ignored an authority's two other roles of regulating affairs within a town by making bye-laws and of publicly representing the community's views. The town consequently was left without a corporate voice during its formative years when decisions were taken by others which shaped the town's future and left after-effects still discernible after 150 years. In particular, the decision of Rathdown Board of Guardians to locate its workhouse at Loughlinstown rather than at Bray, and the decision of the Dublin and Wicklow Railway Company to locate its track between the town and sea-front, rather than west of the urban area, had an adverse long term impact on the future municipality.[3]

When Town Commissioners were again proposed at a public meeting in 1857, circumstances had changed utterly. Population increased from 3,169 in 1841 to 4,182 in 1861, a trend which would continue – see Table 1; the railway had arrived, bringing tourists, 'excursionists' and commuters to the town; a sense of investment opportunity and optimism for the future had developed. The proposals were approved unanimously. The town's 'KCIs' (Key Community Influencers) were present, including Peter Warburton Jackson, a landowner, John Quin Junior, hotelier and developer, and Edward Breslin, hotelier and entrepreneur. The railway company's representative, Dr. Waller, lent support, but admitted that the company had petitioned to have the railway excluded from the town. The railway's unwillingness to contribute financially to the town as ratepayers, was to be a continuing source of tension.[4]

Table 1. Population of Bray 1841–1901[5]

Year	Population	% Growth
1841	3,169	–
1851	3,156	–0.41
1861	4,182	32.51
1871	6,087	45.55
1881	6,535	7.36
1891	6,888	5.40
1901	7,424	7.78

By now the 'package' on offer to towns, was the Towns Improvement (Ireland) Act 1854, containing, like its predecessor, a menu of provisions and powers which were typically required by residents of towns seeking corporate government. It was enhanced, compared with the 1828 Act, by developments in political thought which resulted in a wider franchise, enhanced powers, higher spending limits, and improved management procedures.[6]

The Act enabled towns to spend money on services such as street cleaning, lighting, water supply, fire fighting, sewers, sanitary expenses etc. But it did more: it provided for public order as well as public services, with provisions for controlling through prosecution in the courts, a long list of minor offences – from releasing unmuzzled ferocious dogs to displaying goods on footpaths; from 'acts contrary to public decency' to the dumping of 'dirt, dung, litter or ashes'. It also permitted the making of bye-laws by the Commissioners to control activities such as cars for hire and public bathing.[7]

The electorate was relatively broadly based, consisting of occupiers of premises of £4 poor law valuation or more, and lessors of property of £50 valuation or over – if resident within five miles of the town. Qualifications for candidates for the Commissioners were £12 and £50 respectively. Expenditure was capped at 1s. 0d. in the £1, or 1s. 6d. if water was supplied.[8] The limits on spending and the range of powers may have proved adequate in stable communities with few ambitions, but for an aspiring township like Bray, with a rapidly rising population, a port, considerable inward investment and a growing tourist industry, the spending limits were extremely restricting.

The first board of Commissioners was elected in November 1857. They consisted of the earl of Meath, three other property owners, three business people, two doctors, two hoteliers and the railway company's representative – creating a potential for tension between the different economic interests.[9] Over the next ten years, this body carried out the business of the town, providing services, making bye-laws and representing public opinion – or rather the opinion of the property owners – particularly with regard to the enclosure of Bray Commons by the Bray Commons Commissioners.[10]

In defining the boundaries for the Town Commissioners in 1857, the promoters had limited the urban area to Big Bray except for the undeveloped Lower Commons to the north of the river. This implied a desire both to control the port, and to exclude the poor 'town' of Little Bray, which was presumably seen as a potential burden on the rates. A proposed boundary extension in 1865 – subsequently incorporated in the Bray Township Act of 1866 – to take in Little Bray, Ravenswell and Old Connaught in County Dublin may have been prompted by the town incurring a role north of the river after the Commons was enclosed. The simultaneous extension into Ardmore, Oldcourt and Newcourt areas suggests also a desire to extend the town's rating base, to provide space for further development, and to control the entire sea front.

This desire to extend the town, reflected the ambitions of the more adventurous civic leaders, who were to promote their own Bray Improvement Bill within ten years of the establishment of the Town Commissioners.[11]

BRAY TOWNSHIP ACT 1866

One major frustration of this period, shared with other developing townships, was the need to go cap in hand to the county grand jury, for funds for a wide range of improvement works, such as flagging of footpaths in the Main Street or improving the river mouth. The town paid county cess to the grand jury (£1,500 in 1865), and felt that they only recovered a fraction of this sum for works needed to be carried out within the town. There was talk of 'securing to the township the expenditure of their own money' which led to the proposal for securing a special Township Act for Bray.[12] Interestingly, the board of Town Commissioners did not corporately promote the new Township Bill. It was promoted independently by three of the entrepreneurial group of

Commissioners, William Dargan, Edward Breslin and P.W. Jackson, while the Board itself opposed it, then proclaimed neutrality, then resumed opposition.[13]

While the seeking of independence from the grand jury was in itself non-controversial, the Bill also proposed powers to provide a promenade pier, a sea wall and sea defences, baths and wash-houses, a town hall, fire engines, market house, regulation of markets and fairs, and the building of an important link road. These were purely enabling powers, not mandatory obligations. The promoters also wanted to increase expenditure limits, to increase the township area, and to impose a more restricted franchise than had previously existed for the town. Some of these proposals provoked controversy.[14]

Objections centred on the potential increase in taxation, on the extension of boundaries (which also had implications for taxation), and on the question of franchise. Chairman of the Commissioners, John Quin, the hotelier, was resolute in opposition. He proclaimed 'higher taxes would discourage people from engaging residences [in Bray]'. He decried lack of consultation, as all objectors do. John Kingsmill T.C. foresaw the destruction of Bray. The earl of Meath was generally lukewarm – he argued that commercial enterprise, not the town's ratepayers, should provide the promenade pier 'for ladies to walk on'. He also threatened opposition in parliament to any interference with his rights as lord of the manor, to the control of, and the collection of tolls from, the markets and fairs.[15] Little Bray ratepayers sought powers to improve the river mouth, with the cost to be charged to the beneficiaries from such works.[16] The thrust of these arguments indicated that taxation was not yet seen as a valid means of transferring wealth. Everyone guarded his own self interest.

P.W. Jackson moved to find a compromise. He attended and spoke at public meetings of ratepayers, and produced alternative drafts of the Bill to meet objections. These included dropping the promenade pier proposal, modifying the market provisions, limiting the taxation and borrowing powers, and including extra powers to protect the river mouth with new embankments.[17] Not satisfied, the Commissioners lodged a petition in parliament against the Bill, the promoters in turn opposed the petition, and the Bill went through, incorporating the amendments lodged by Jackson. The town had to pay £180 to its own solicitors for opposing the bill with extra promoters' costs to be added later.[18]

The question of franchise had been particularly controversial. The Little Bray ratepayers sought a wider, not a narrower franchise as proposed: the *Bray Gazette*, on the other hand reflected the bias of 'those who mattered', in favour of the property owner over the consumer of services, when it editorialised: 'we cannot approve of the principle of small cotters ruling the rates for large property owners. Bray ... demands a more liberal and enlightened policy than it is likely to attain under a £5 rating constituency'.[19] In the event, the Act, as adopted by parliament, contained a reactionary provision which limited the electoral franchise to occupiers with property of £7 or greater valuation compared with the previous £4 limit. The qualification for standing for Commissioner was increased from £12 to £30.[20] The effect of this was to stem the growth of popular participation in town government. The property quali-fication for Commissioners was subsequently reduced by the Town Councils and Local Boards Act 1880 to the same level as that of electors.[21]

The controversy spotlighted a number of divisions within the community. There was Main Street and Little Bray against the Esplanade, the traditional town against the tourist/development lobby, the land owners on the periphery against the townspeople, the developing town against the earl of Meath over markets. Most noticeable of all however, was the conflict of interest between the entrepreneurs and other ratepayers, which was part of a long-continuing saga. A new element had also emerged in town politics: the Little Bray Ratepayers' meeting was dominated by car owners, grocers, vintners and a timber merchant, forming a counter-balance to the more middle-class-orientated entrepreneurs.[22]

The new Commissioners met for the first time in September 1866 with fifteen Commissioners statutorily nominated but subject to subsequent re-election. There were six property owners, two hoteliers, two professionals, a builder, an entrepreneur, a miller and a publican. The majority were Protestants. One third of the Commissioners were to retire in rotation each year, prevent-ing any total rout of outgoing members and giving the body a stability and continuity.[23]

This exercise of promoting the Improvement Bill, besides illustrating the inadequacies of standardised urban legislation, demonstrated the divisions in the town, and the machinery used to integrate the different views through compromise. Despite having to compromise on the original proposals how-ever, the promoters succeeded in removing some of the legislative constraints on the town's expansion and development.

CENTRAL CONTROL

At the very time when enhanced powers and higher expenditure limits promised a greater freedom for local government in Bray, political thinking in London was tending towards greater control from the centre. While boards of guardians, due to the philosophy of Edwin Chadwick, had been tightly controlled since their inception, town legislation had been more relaxed.[24] But in 1866, the Sanitation Act introduced a new concept – the role of local government as an agent for central policy.[25] In addition, the parliament's interest in social and economic life, the desire for some uniformity, and the need for ministerial responsibility for defects in local government, led to a sea-change towards centralisation.[26] In Ireland, the change was first noticed in the

Local Government (Ireland) Act 1871[27] and the Local Government Board
(Ireland) Act 1872 which established the Local Government Board, as a controlling mechanism over local authorities.[28]

In Bray, one section of the 1871 Act, (section 12) was to have a far-reaching
negative effect on the Town Commissioners' attitudes to their work. Previously
the commissioners' accounts were audited by two of their number who reported
back to the board of Commissioners. Section 12 however, provided for an
auditor appointed by the Local Government Board to examine all the accounts
of the township and

> disallow and strike out . . . all payments . . . contrary to law, or which
> he deems to be unfounded and shall surcharge upon the person making
> . . . the illegal payment . . . and certify the same to be due from such
> person . . .

In other words the auditor 'without dispensations or allowance', had to bill
Commissioners personally if they signed any cheques which he considered
illegal.[29]

While one cannot argue against the principle that one person may not spend
another's money without authority, the concept of illegality was extremely
wide.[30] Given the scope for a wide interpretation by the auditor and given his
autocratic power, some nervousness might be expected of any Commissioners.
In Bray, however, they had a traumatic personal experience of the new audit
system at an early date. The difficulties were not generally foreseen. Some people
in Ireland had argued in favour of the new audit.[31] The Bray Commissioners
'adopted' the new system, though it was in fact mandatory.

The problem in Bray started on 5 June 1874 when the local government
auditor visited the town to audit the 1873 accounts. He was met by a group
of 'influential ratepayers' who pointed out possible illegal payments totalling
over £1,000.[32] The Commissioners responded quickly. The town clerk wrote
to the earl of Meath saying a surcharge was expected and £495 of the queried
cheques 'had your Lordship's signature'. Lord Meath immediately sent for his
solicitor, Octavius O'Brien, 'to take measures without delay'; telegrams were
passed; Octavius, fully briefed, met George Finlay the auditor. O'Brien reported
back that most of the expenditure could be defended but he referred to the
threat posed by the 'agitation now being attempted as per *Saunder's Newsletter*'.[33]

There were three main problems to be faced. Firstly, £1,000 was spent to
complete the very important final section of the Dargle Road (then New
Bridge Road) near Bray Bridge. The 1866 Bray Township Act had authorised
the building of the road within six years (to 23 July 1872). Due to legal
difficulties, construction ran into 1873. The auditor at the public hearing ruled
the 1873 expenditure illegal, and said he would have to disallow it (i.e. charge
it to the Commissioners personally). He would consider it further before

enforcing payment. There was apparently some connivance between O'Brien and the auditor, because O'Brien confided in a *private* letter to Lord Meath that he had intended pleading alternative authority from a previous grand jury presentment of the expenditure, but found the presentment defective; that the auditor himself had carefully 'avoided' producing the defective document at the hearing; that he (O'Brien) had 'greatest difficulty' preventing the town surveyor, who was unaware of the defect, from referring to the presentment at the hearing. O'Brien believed that covering authority could be got from the grand jury by a bill in chancery at a later time. In the meantime it 'should be kept a profound secret' until 'the matter passes'.[34] Secondly, a £25 payment to the grand jury towards the County Surveyor's salary was deemed 'a double payment' (a payment in addition to the county cess) and was disallowed. It was refunded later by the grand jury, so the charge was not enforced. Thirdly, sewerage connections totalling £289 were disallowed. They should have been paid out of a special sewer rate chargeable to beneficiaries instead of from the town rate. Later the Commissioners successfully appealed that these were paid out of borrowing and *not* out of the town rate – even though the effect was the same – charging all ratepayers for the cost of sewers rather than those who had specifically benefited from them. In the end the Commissioners escaped nearly all the surcharges on technicalities.[35]

These examples illustrate the financial risk to the unpaid commissioners every time they signed a cheque. They also illustrate the powerful tool in the hands of even one negatively-minded ratepayer against the spending of 'his' money, particularly as Section 12 provided specifically for a writ of certiorari (a judicial review) if anyone was aggrieved by an auditor's decision. Such a system to 'protect' the ratepayer was by definition a system to inhibit creativity in action. Much later, it inhibited the emergence of the 'development corporation' concept of a local authority. The audit system must have represented a powerful disincentive for potential Commissioners, as did the political hassle, the restricted qualifications for members and the day-time meetings (particularly in what was becoming a commuter town). The result was a limited pool from which to elect the town leadership and a consequent reduction in level of skills and performance. Richard R. Wingfield J.P., however, considered the franchise far too wide, thereby ensuring that 'gentlemen' could not be elected.[36]

A RATEPAYERS' LOBBY

Meanwhile the ratepayers were not inactive. They established a Ratepayers' Association and started collecting subscriptions. They had the support of *Saunder's Newsletter* and planned to comment on potential surcharges. If dissatisfied with an auditor's decision, they would argue a case at the Queen's Bench. Bray, they said, suffered from enormous taxation; the New Bridge

Road should have been paid for by the grand jury. This was the other side of the argument on the paying of county cess at the time of the 1866 Township Bill.[37] They said that the chairman, the earl of Meath only paid £8 rates as he lived outside the town at Kilruddery, and he was therefore little affected by taxation.[38] In addition, they determined to seek an injunction against the Commissioners who were threatening to resign en masse, thereby leaving the town with no local authority. They would call up voluntary subscriptions for improving the Bray River which had not been followed up. They would investigate past expenditure, particularly with respect to whether Commissioners owned those houses which had been served with water and sewerage. They would insist that only heavy ratepayers of experience be appointed chairmen of the Commissioners in future.[39]

The auditorial incident occurred in June 1874. In October of that year one third of the Commissioners came up for re-election and some new names appeared on the Board – Henry Warburton, Thomas Purcell, James Murphy, and Edward Rooney, all of whom had been listed as attending the audit as ratepayers.[40] The earl of Meath resigned both as chairman and Commissioner. Richard Cuthbert, another 'ratepayer', was co-opted a Commissioner in his place. James Murphy, in proposing him, referred to 'the toadism and sycophancy' of the late board. Edward Rooney said he had been misrepresented in his previous criticism of the earl. If Lord Meath had done 'very little for the township he did no harm'.[41]

This partial coup of ratepayers against the old guard was seen by some as a loss of 'respectability'. Edward Breslin, a founding father of the Commissioners, stated 'I do not think it was ever the intention to have such a class of men as were then on the Board acting as Town Commissioners for such a town as Bray'. He said that James Murphy having been fired as town clerk, after a 'he goes or I go' ultimatum from the earl of Meath, was elected as a Commissioner, as were Edward Rooney, tailor and pawnbroker, and others who had formed a clique and caused the earl and several 'respectable' members of the Commissioners to resign.[42] Breslin fought back through the courts. He had Richard Cuthbert unseated from the chairmanship on the basis of illegality in form of election; he then had him removed from membership on the grounds of contracting with the Commissioners in the name of his servant. Breslin got a judgement against Cuthbert for £650, a very considerable sum. Two further Commissioners were co-opted to fill vacancies. Breslin threatened further legal action and they declined to take up their seats.[43]

THE 1876 ROYAL COMMISSION OF INQUIRY

The 1876 Royal Commission of Inquiry, was a dramatic event in the history of the Commissioners. In that year a Select Committee of the House of

Commons was established to examine and report on local government and taxation of Irish towns. The Committee, in turn, sought and received a report from a Royal Commission based on evidence it had taken around the country, together with a special overview report from an inspector of the Irish Local Government Board. While the three reports were couched in global terms, specific problems in specific towns were also addressed by the Royal Commission in their taking of evidence.

In the case of Bray, there were routine complaints about water supplies and gas lighting but also there were two dramatic interventions. The first occurred when the local medical officer of health unexpectedly 'dropped a bomb' with trenchant criticism of the sanitary situation in Bray.[44]

The second element of drama resulted from James Murphy's allegations of waste, corruption and jobbery against the Commissioners. Within a few years, James Murphy had been fired as the town clerk, become a founder member of the Ratepayers' Association, been elected a member of the Commissioners, been elected its chairman, and resigned from both.[45]

At the inquiry he alleged waste and discrimination in favour of the richer areas at the expense of Little Bray. But he made numerous allegations of favouritism in prioritising of works to benefit Commissioners personally – placing kerbs around Brennan's Terrace and Brennan's Parade owned by Charles Dufresne T.C.; building a sewer to the house of Henry Kingsmill T.C.; laying a gas main to John Bruce T.C.'s isolated house at Crowbank; providing sewers to P.W. Jackson T.C.'s cesspool, installing a public light outside the home of John O'Neill T.C. He particularly attacked Edward Breslin for having 'road scrapings' brought to his own private road and thence to his farm, for drawing seaweed across the esplanade (against the rules) for his farm rather than to the People's Park, but more particularly he attacked the exceptionally high standard of maintenance of that part of the esplanade opposite Breslin's Hotel. Finally, he alleged different standards of rate collecting – some Commissioners had not paid rates while he himself was summoned only three days after the rates were struck.[46]

Simon Doyle, the rate collector involved, was called for examination. His response was pathetic. He replied in monosyllables or he failed to answer. He was son of a Commissioner and he was under the legal age when appointed.[47] He was a boy in a man's job: to give an eighteen year old the responsibility of collecting rates, a post requiring ability to apply strong statutory powers with discretion, was asking just too much. He appeared to be a person intimidated by the Commissioners and by the job. He was ineffective and disorganised.[48]

Breslin and others then responded to Murphy's allegations. Breslin said that he had been asked to take the road scrapings onto his land to avoid having to dump them further away. They were of no value. Seaweed had to be removed before it decayed and he bought it from those who gathered it. Anyone who bought it, drew it across the esplanade. More maintenance was needed outside his hotel than elsewhere as the storms hit hardest near that point. The sewer to Kingsmill's estate served other houses and it was part of the deal that Kingsmill's roads were to become public. Jackson had convinced the Commissioners that they should pipe the cesspool. Brennan's Terrace was only one of the areas where kerbs were laid. Bruce paid one third of the cost of his gas main, on similar terms to elsewhere. And John O'Neill according to Breslin, was a man incapable of jobbery.[49]

How did the Commissioners emerge from the charges? It is difficult to draw conclusions after 120 years. Murphy who made the allegations had a personal vendetta to pursue. The Royal Commission reported that the allegations were not substantiated.[50] Yet there is a difference between proving guilt and proving innocence. In the nineteenth century the allocation of funds for extension of services to different parts of the town was as open to suspicion as the rezoning activities of any local authority in the twentieth century. Whatever is done, someone will be favoured against others. It is true that in Bray suspicion was rife about doing favours for friends. Yet the system provided for doing deals in the sense of bargaining on contributions towards services. Certainly a gas main to Bruce's house would have been hard to justify given its isolation; doing a deal with Kingsmill to lay a sewer only if he allowed the Commissioners to take his estate in charge seems to give him two benefits rather than one. Priority for kerbing of Brennan's Terrace could be argued, but not for Brennan's Parade, the laneway at the rear. Jackson's cesspool was fed from Hudson's Terrace, a slum area adjoining his residence and draining it was certainly a valid public health exercise. Breslin and Dufresne, as owners of Breslin's and the International Hotels respectively, stood to benefit disproportionately from all expenditure on the esplanade, particularly Breslin, and while he was correct in arguing that his section of the esplanade suffered most (and still does) from storm damage, the constant hints and allegations regarding provision of services to benefit him particularly, appear to have some substance.[51]

The enquiry uncovered one clear-cut case of dishonesty on the Council staff – the road overseer digging out his own potatoes with the help of the Commissioners' workmen. He may have been the fall-guy; the incident was raised by Breslin in response to a question on whether work had been done by Commissioners' staff for the personal benefit of the Commissioners. The reply had the effect of 'changing the subject' to a new line of questioning.[52]

On the general grounds of corruption, then, one can conclude that although the charges against the Commissioners were officially 'unsubstantiated', the 'town fathers' were not proven innocent, and considerable suspicion of sleaze must remain. But no heads rolled, and after the trauma of the audit, the ratepayers' coup, and the public enquiry, the Board settled down to a more relaxed mode. Indeed, on occasions elections were unopposed.[53]

LORD BRABAZON RETURNS HOME

Trouble was brewing which was to change permanently the town's relationship with the lord of the manor. It will be recalled that during the ratepayers' coup in 1874 the earl of Meath resigned from both chairmanship and membership of the Commissioners. Some like Richard R. Wingfield J.P. said he was 'kicked out'.[54] Throughout the period, the question of ownership of rights to market tolls was a matter of continual contention between the Commissioners and the earl. The breakdown in relations between the Meath family and the town occurred however on two separate unexpected issues.

In 1875, following the death of Matthew O'Reilly Dease, Ravenswell was put up for sale and it was bought by the earl of Meath for his son and heir, Lord Brabazon, who had spent most of his life abroad. In April 1878 Lord Brabazon wrote to the Commissioners asking them to remove the stones and gravel dumped on Ravenswell Road or he would take legal action. They said they would do so and put it in repair. He thanked them and said he was restoring the estate, ending the practice of O'Reilly Dease of letting it become a 'common place of convenience'.

Next Lord Brabazon put gates across the road which was the only access from Little Bray to the shore north of the river mouth. The Commissioners wrote to him referring to memorials of protest from the residents against the closing of the right of way. Desultory correspondence went on for over a year. Octavius O'Brien, advised Lord Meath that there was no right of way due to a Landed Estates Court decision.[55] The Commissioners' legal advice was that the road was not included in the Court's ruling. Backed by this advice, the Commissioners disputed Lord Brabazon's title; he asked to see their legal advice; they responded that it was 'unusual' but they would swap respective advices. There was no further request.[56]

The Commissioners decided to force Lord Brabazon to act and told him that on a given day and at a given time an official would enter the gate at Ravenswell Road and proceed to the shore to test Lord Brabazon's claim. No violence would be offered and they could later meet in court. The day arrived. Octavius O'Brien, with two or three men, stood behind the padlocked gate. The roads inspector and a horse and cart arrived – together with a labourer with a sledge hammer who broke the lock, opened the gate and led the cart through. The gate remained open. The people reclaimed the right of way to and from the beach, but some turned in horses, donkeys and goats to graze on the grass margins and feed on the ornamental trees recently planted by Lord Brabazon. O'Brien wrote saying that he would accept the proposal to let the courts decide. The Commissioners suggested a settlement. Lord Brabazon gave in as graciously as possible. While repeating his legal claim, he would dedicate the road to the town as it was 'of great advantage to the people of Bray'. He would replace the vandalised trees himself.[57]

Lord Brabazon lost the argument but he lost more. His first public involvement in municipal affairs unnecessarily isolated him from the townspeople and created enemies at a time when Bray, for the only time in the Victorian period, was about to become party-politicised. The error of judgement may have arisen from Lord Brabazon's absence abroad for most of his life, from his lack of contact with the populous and from the unreal atmosphere which was created on celebratory occasions like his marriage in 1868 when bonfires blazed, and his coach was physically dragged up the avenue of Kilruddery by the tenantry.[58] As a result of this dispute, he was left at a disadvantage when the next more serious event took place.

THE TOWN HALL/MARKET HOUSE

Within months of the Ravenswell Road incident, Lord Brabazon offered to build a market house for the town, and to lease it to the Commissioners at a subsidised rent. He confided to his solicitor – no doubt sincerely – 'Lady Brabazon and I wish to do a benefit for the town of Bray'. But there is evidence that Lord Brabazon was also trying to enhance his own image in the town, by reflecting his power and station. Many stained glass windows, a carved fireplace and the ornamental fountain outside, incorporated Brabazon family armorial decorations, designed after much consultation between Lord Brabazon and his architect. It was to be a building 'worthy of the town and ourselves'.[59]

Lord Brabazon lacked what to-day would be called 'the community development approach'. He himself decided what was needed by the townspeople; he himself got the building designed, incorporating a town hall as well as the market house. This caused the cost to spiral from the £2,720 tendered in 1879 to the £6,359 in the final account, requiring an increased, though still subsidised, rent.[60] Heretofore the Town Commissioners were based at the court house.

The first problem occurred when the Commissioners sought powers in Parliament in early 1881, for operating the market house and town hall – thereby usurping the earl of Meath's market rights. He demanded the withdrawal of the market proposals. Then the Commissioners queried a proposed rent of £80 per annum, reflecting increased costs, instead of the £50 already agreed. Lord Brabazon was irate. He told his agent in London 'I am sick of the whole affair . . . Lady Brabazon and I, after the manner in which our offer has been received are not at all anxious to build. We thought we were doing a favour'. He told the Commissioners that if they could get money elsewhere on better terms they should do so. The Commissioners backed off, 'content to carry out his Lordship's requirements'. They passed a resolution of praise and gratitude to both the earl of Meath and Lord Brabazon.[61] The offending clauses were removed from the bill.

1. Bray Town Hall

Construction work was almost complete when the next conflict occurred. Lord Meath, as owner of the land, introduced four requirements: to have six days use of the main hall each year; to exclude political or religious meetings; to secure from the Commissioners a free supply of water for the fountain; to retain the coffee-stall franchise in the market.[62] These requests were relatively minor, but a dynamic had already built up which led to excesses on both sides. On the one hand Lord Brabazon was being stirred up by his architect: 'the Irish people . . . not worthy of the fountain'; 'I am sorry it is not going to where it is better deserved, as the people in Bray have treated you very badly'.[63] On the side of the Commissioners and townspeople, the political situation nationally was for the first time raising the temperature in Bray. Bray had never previously been deeply involved in nationalist issues: for example, the Fenian period had passed without incident. Yet the people were aware of developments in national politics: in 1869 an attendance of 20,000, mainly outsiders, demonstrated in Purcell's field in favour of the release of political prisoners; the effigy of Judge William Kehoe (who lived outside Bray) was burnt here in 1872 – as elsewhere – after his unseating of a Home Rule candidate in the Galway election; over 12,000 attended an amnesty meeting in Bray in 1873.[64] Nationalist politics had, however, caused few ripples in the Commissioners until around 1880, though there had been an increasing number of Catholic nationalist Commissioners. The Land League was formed in 1879, and the 'Michael Davitt Branch' was founded in Bray in October 1881.[65] Its 'declaration of principles' stressing the rights of the people to the land, had the potential for causing trouble between Bray and Kilruddery. Lord Brabazon's closing of Ravenswell Road played into the hands of his political enemies. The Commissioners were roughly split down the middle between Conservatives and nationalists reflecting the outside tensions. The Conservatives had a small majority.

When Lord Meath sought the four additional clauses in the draft lease of the town hall/market house, the Commissioners balked. Breslin however pushed through an approval, resulting in the fight being transferred from the board room to a new arena – community politics.[66] By the end of 1883, Lord Brabazon accused the town of ingratitude and threatened legal action. A poster appeared around the town from 'a nationalist ratepayer' calling for a boycott of the town hall. An anonymous letter-writer – 'Nipo' – wrote to the *Freeman's Journal* reminding the noblemen that 'this is 1884 not 1784' and threatening an injunction against the Commissioners. Lord Brabazon's solicitors replied at length in a letter typical of the establishment in a 'City Hall v. People' controversy – at length, in legal terms, unemotional, stressing the benevolence of their client, and stating his reasonable position. Very Reverend Dean Lee P.P. led a deputation to the Town Commissioners with a memorial of protest. Unlike the solicitors' letter, theirs was typical of a 'Peoples' power' approach – political and emotive – 'he demands baronial rights', 'an obnoxious ascendancy to last for the next 900 years' (the length of the proposed lease); 'taunted by Lord Brabazon with ingratitude'. But the insult that hurt most was 'the heart of Lord Meath is as Orange as the heart of Lord Rossmore – a magistrate degraded for disloyalty to his office'. On a more practical level they said the building was 'costly in its decorations . . . totally unsuited to the needs of the town'. The town needed a large hall for public meetings and concerts, and dealers needed a shed in which to buy and sell potatoes. These could be provided at little cost.[67]

A counter-demonstration was organised in Breslin's Hotel to sympathise with the earl of Meath. Their chief speaker was the town's second parish priest, Rev. J. Healy, P.P. of Little Bray who avoided joining in the controversy, but praised Lords Meath and Brabazon. His appearance was by no means considered to have been a breaking of ranks as he was already well renowned for moving in high society.[68] Supporters called it a large and influential meeting; critics said about fourteen attended. Lord Meath's supporters organised a memorial signed by 220 people, and sent a deputation to the Commissioners to get them to accept the new conditions.[69] Mr. A. Burton and Fr. Lee led opposing deputations, each presenting a memorial to the Commissioners. The first stressed the high rateable value of their supporters' property; the other the high number of signatories, 303 against 220; each queried the validity of the others' signatures.[70]

Edward Breslin said he had a 'two-fold' capacity, which was quoted back as a 'two-faced' capacity.[71] This was nearer the truth, as he had written confidentially to Lord Brabazon with personal comments on Fr. Lee's list of signatures, and on the various Commissioners – particularly in regard to who would support Lord Meath in a showdown. He submitted an off-the-record suggested compromise. He was keeping the document secret for the time, allowing 'the agitation to subside and abide a better opportunity when the information may be found extremely valuable'.[72]

From design stage, the architect had been afraid of vandalism, particularly to the stained glass windows and the fountain, but in January 1884 feelings were running so high that 'a guard of constabulary' was placed on the town hall around the clock.[73] But already moves were afoot to reach a compromise. A deputation of Commissioners visited Lord Brabazon's solicitors in February. John Plunkett, a leading nationalist Commissioner, wrote to Lord Brabazon a long, moderate, respectful, reasonable, conciliatory letter. Further correspondence was exchanged, and agreement was reached in April whereby Lord Brabazon yielded on Lord Meath's claim to rights for the six days use of the hall, the free supply of water for the fountain and the coffee-stall franchise, but won his point of no political or religious meetings. After this, Plunkett, an argumentative individual reverted to form and, having voted initially for the compromise and proposed a vote of thanks to Lord Brabazon, he demanded at the next meeting, that the deal be rescinded on the grounds that there had been a misunderstanding.[74] Breslin was aggrieved that the six days use of the hall had been conceded by Lord Brabazon despite his own stand against conceding it. He called personally to Lord Brabazon's solicitors to complain – a call which cost Lord Brabazon the price of a legal consultation. The solicitor suggested that Lord Meath should send Breslin 'some friendly letter'.[75]

At the height of the dispute, in mid-January 1885, William O'Brien M.P. and Timothy Harrington M.P., leaders of the National League, addressed a crowd in Bray while on their way to a demonstration in Roundwood. They proclaimed that the people of Bray, 'once the stronghold of whiggery or rather of toryism' had at last begun to think for themselves. They hoped that the people of Bray would be emancipated from subjection to Kilruddery. The signatories of an address presented to the leaders by the Bray branch of the League included in the main, the names of past, present and future Commissioners – John Plunkett, Martin Langton, James Doyle, James Robinson, Thomas Clifford, Peter Cunningham, Patrick Tierney, Joseph Coghlan, Patrick O'Connor, Garret Nolan, Nicholas Mooney and others.[76] This meeting reflected the growth of nationalist feeling in Bray, the influence of the National League on the Commissioners and the symbolic value of the dispute with Kilruddery.

Feeling among non-nationalists was also running high and a branch of the Irish Loyal and Patriotic Union was formed by – among others – Lord Meath and Edward Breslin in October 1885.[77] The terms 'unionist' and 'nationalist' are used in this work in a general sense.

While this dispute ended in compromise, it represented the final participation of Kilruddery in the municipal affairs of Bray, after a period of 275 years.

That end was, however, probably inevitable with the subsequent arrival in 1899 of a more democratic system of local government.

The Municipal Boundaries Commission (Ireland), held a public inquiry in Bray, and in 112 other towns, in 1879. Their terms of reference involved reviewing the boundaries and the taxation of towns. Boundary extensions had occasionally been discussed in Bray over the years. It was a complex problem for Commissioners to calculate whether the rate receipts from an added area would exceed the cost of providing services there, just as it was for individuals to calculate whether the services to them would be worth the rates payable. Lord Meath's request in 1872 for the extension of the town to Kilruddery, had been opposed on financial grounds by existing ratepayers, and was rejected. At the time of the Boundaries Commission, the Town Commissioners were undecided on the issue. Breslin himself suggested an extension to Tillystown (Shankill) – two miles away. At the end of the day, the Commissioners recommended extension to Kilruddery and Old Connaught – but these recommendations were never implemented.[78]

The next strategic event, was the Bray Township Extension Bill 1881. This envisaged not just the extension of the town as far as the Shanganagh stream, three miles away, but the construction of a sea wall to protect the Esplanade, the building of the town hall, market house and a harbour, together with ancillary financial and other provisions. There was great opposition to the proposed extension, from both ratepayers and potential ratepayers, and, to certain of the provisions regarding markets, from Lord Meath.[79] The Report of the Municipal Boundaries Commission recommending an extension had not yet been published and the Bill, as the Bray Township Act 1881, went through without the offending provisions.

The ending of the town hall dispute did not end the dissension in the board room. There was a period of some years of aggression, antagonism and abuse – not in the board room alone, but also in the courts of law. Breslin, assisted by Thomas Craig, a Commissioner and solicitor, pursued a legal offensive against their political enemies, challenging, for various reasons, the election or co-option to the chair, of Peter Cunningham, James Robinson, Thomas Moyne M.P., Nicholas Mooney, Joseph Coghlan, and T.A. Byrne (all nationalists). A fear of Breslin's wealth and determination, of Craig's profession and of unionist financial backing for the litigation, resulted in some of those challenged backing down and resigning in face of the threats of legal action and costs. A fund was established to indemnify nationalist Commissioners against legal costs.[80]

Joseph Coghlan had resigned when challenged that he had sold bathing dresses, valued £2 to the Commissioners, while he was a Commissioner himself; James Robinson was removed because of a defect in his co-option.[81] The Martin Langton case, however, was the cause célèbre. He ran an ironmonger's shop and, while he was a Commissioner, the Commissioners' staff had purchased requirements there. Langton defeated Breslin for chairman in October 1886, the first time that a nationalist won the post. Breslin made the complaint that Langton was disqualified. He resigned as Commissioner on 20th December 1886 after taking legal advice and Breslin tried to stop his resignation until after the court case. 'He has nothing to resign'. Langton pleaded lack of knowledge of any illegality on his part and pleaded that Breslin had sold the Ladies' Baths to the Commissioners, as well as conniving at contracts with various Board members. In court, Breslin won his case with costs.[82]

The court action was merely a reflection of the disarray in the board room. Press reports referred to 'squabble', 'emphatic talking', 'warm language', 'general din', 'usual dispute as to who should take the chair' and so on. Abuse was hurled – 'falsehood', 'threat to break nose', 'treason', 'slave', 'the little chairman in the little tall hat' (Breslin of Langton). Party politics prevailed. A motion 'dishonouring the Queen' was passed 'unanimously' after the unionists had left one meeting. At other times, unionists walked out. Their allegations of National League influence were not denied. Business was difficult to transact. There were disputes over chairmanship, over signing of minutes and over other legalistic and procedural matters.[83] Robert McAlpine, of McAlpines the Glasgow-based civil engineering firm which built the promenade, arrived at one meeting personally to demand £1,500 payment, and entered the chamber in the midst of a political melee. The Board immediately went into committee to continue the squabble so McAlpine had to click his heels in the hallway until he was readmitted after things had calmed down.[84]

By 1888 there were signs of matters becoming more stable. In the October election for chairman, Langton (once again a Commissioner) beat Breslin (outgoing) and a 'nationalist' vote of thanks was passed to the outgoing chairman, which Breslin graciously accepted. A year later, Langton proposed that he would give way to another – younger – nationalist, James Hennessy, to effusive praise from the unionist members.[85]

The earlier lack of unity in the board room had meant little development of services during the 1880s. The hassle in the boardroom and the decline in the 'respectability' of Commissioners must have been disincentives for some future Commissioners, because 'respectability' was an obsession of the middle classes.

RETURN OF RELATIVE CALM

The board room relapsed into a period of relative calm. Three acts of parliament were secured by the township, in 1890, 1895 and 1896. In 1890, an extension of the statutory time limit for constructing harbour works, a promenade pier and an outfall sewer (originally authorised in 1881) was secured, and authority was obtained to extend the sea wall or promenade. The Commissioners also secured ancillary powers to borrow for consolidation of debt, and for making a harbour rate etc. This was the Bray Township Act of 1890. The 1895 act of the same name gave power to raise further money for the works proposed, to extend the harbour area and to acquire land to provide an electricity supply. The actual power to provide electricity followed under the Electric Lighting Orders Confirmation (No. 3) Act 1896.[86]

In the early 1890s the unionist population were still in the majority and there tended to be a unionist chairman. However, as already noted, unionists and nationalists were not monolithic groupings. In October 1894 Breslin's chairmanship was proposed by the outgoing unionist, Henry Jackson, and seconded by Martin Langton, the nationalist. Some unionists wanted 'a younger man' but, despite taunts from Jackson, they failed to propose a name, five of them walking out leaving the other four unionists to join with the nationalists in electing Breslin. Similarly, the nationalists had their mavericks – for example, Richard Clifton topped the poll in nationalist Little Bray to show that this ward was 'not impregnable' for the established representatives.[87]

In 1896 Edward Breslin by then aged seventy-eight and in decline, refused the position of chairman. A new unionist leader, Sir Henry Cochrane, took over. In April 1897 Breslin resigned as Commissioner. Martin Langton the nationalist, led an all party deputation asking him to reconsider his decision. Breslin, far from well and speaking with emotion agreed to continue. He died in office on 7 June 1897, after forty years of almost continuous service as a Commissioner, many of them as chairman.[88]

Edward Breslin, now generally forgotten, was undoubtedly one of the 'founding fathers' of modern Bray. Son of a 'small farmer' from Baltinglass, he rose through jobs of carter and house steward, to be 'discovered' by William Dargan. Dargan gave him the position of caterer for the Dublin Exhibition of 1853. Under Dargan's influence, he opened the refreshment room at the new Bray railway station. He built the first hotel in the town, (apart from the long established Quin's) – Breslin's Royal Marine. Later, he bought Royal Marine Terrace, Fitzwilliam Terrace, Dock Terrace and Carlisle Grounds and had an interest in the International Hotel. The Royal Marine Hotel, however, remained his principal interest.[89] He was one of the entrepreneurial triumvirate with William Dargan and James Brennan who made the pace in the period of the first Commissioners, 1857–1866, which coincided with the boom-time in Bray. He promoted the town as a seaside resort championing the development of the esplanade, the promenade, a promenade pier, the ladies' baths and so on. It can be argued, however, that he thought of Bray exclusively as a holiday town and was more interested in the sea-front than in slum clearance.

He was a man not to be crossed. He was not slow to criticise others. He was litigation-conscious and appeared in court on numerous occasions.[90] His legal disputes with other Commissioners will be recalled. And he was accused of sexual assault in 1884. Shortly after becoming a magistrate, Breslin was accused of assault by Margaret Gaskin 'a quiet looking girl evidently in humble circumstances' ('here follow details unfit for publication') – and of 'putting his hand under my dress' when she called to collect a summons from his hotel.[91] She got a local man 'who sometimes wrote letters for people' to write a statement for her. The local solicitor would not take such a case against the local magistrate so the family got a solicitor in Dublin. She made no complaint to the R.I.C., however. Breslin's case was to deny the assault, suggesting a political motive for making the charge. Breslin was returned for trial on bail by a majority of five magistrates. At Wicklow assizes, the case was dismissed by the jury after ten minutes deliberation. It was unusual at the time for a man of rank to be charged with sexual misconduct, let alone be convicted. The newspaper reports show conflict of evidence but the presiding judge made it clear to the jury that he considered that Breslin should be found not guilty.[92]

Breslin, perhaps because of his humble origin, was wont to curry favour with the aristocracy. He was reported to have changed the name 'Claddagh Terrace' to 'Fitzwilliam Terrace' to please Fitzwilliam Hume M.P. As already noted, he secretly briefed Lord Meath during the town hall dispute. Yet he was distrusted by Lord Meath's solicitor who advised his client 'notwithstanding what Breslin writes I know he has spoken to the contrary'.[93] As a Commissioner, Breslin always claimed to be straight in his dealings, and disputed claims that he benefited improperly when Commissioners' services were being prioritised. In this case he had a point as *any* work near his hotel would benefit him. By the time he retired he would appear to have been well-regarded by most people in the town. Breslin was responsible for much of the town's inward investment of the early sixties; he was a doer during the Commissioners' formative years. Though he resigned with Lord Meath and others in 1874, he returned shortly afterwards and for decades, gave the town government a sense of continuity and stability, in a time of change.

BRAY URBAN DISTRICT COUNCIL

The Town Commissioners were about to be superseded as a result of local government reform. The Local Government Act of 1898 inter alia created democratically elected county councils in lieu of grand juries, and divided the country into district council areas – urban and rural. Bray was to become an urban district. The town boundary was not changed but Little Bray was transferred from County Dublin to County Wicklow. There was little change in basic powers and responsibilities but the franchise was widened to include parliamentary voters (male householders and lodgers) plus women – which in time also widened the pool for Commissioners, as the qualifications for electors and Commissioners were the same.[94]

One might expect that the new council would have been immediately dominated by newly enfranchised nationalists, but an interesting coalition of unionists and existing nationalist members was formed. The 'Progressive Committee' was established including Cochrane, McCormick and McFarland (unionist) and Clifton, Condrin and Langton (nationalist).[95] They swept the boards. In the East Ward they won the first eight seats, John Plunkett, the Ratepayers candidate, getting the last place. In the West Ward they won two out of three seats; in the not-very-establishment-minded Little Bray, they won all three seats. Outgoing chairman John Plunkett, a nationalist who ran as a 'Ratepayer', was aggrieved, alleging 'buying the township' with porter and the 'selection of the chairman at a mixed meeting, at the Royal Hotel'. Plunkett was reminded that he himself formed the first 'combination' in 1873.[96]

J.E. McCormick became first chairman of the urban district council and was succeeded in 1900 by Sir Henry Cochrane. He in turn was succeeded in 1901 by Philip Condrin 'a working man' and former community activist who was elected unanimously, Sir Henry having endorsed him on behalf of the Tories. The Victorian era was over. The same meeting of the Commissioners which elected Condrin, passed a vote of condolence with the king – almost unanimously – on the death of his mother, Queen Victoria.[97]

This examination of the growth of administration in Bray, noted the changes dictated by the central government, as well as the influence of local lobby groups. The dichotomy running over decades between the savers (ratepayers) and spenders was noted. There were, of course, also the divisions on religious and political lines, and those between 'fashionable Bray' interests on the one hand, and Little Bray and poorer districts on the other. National politics, however, impacted strongly in the board room for a short period only, in the early 1880s. And generally the groupings were not monolithic in character, but permitted informal coalitions to be formed as the situation required. There were other pressure groups, like vocational groups (fishermen and car men), and single-issue groups, those opposing the construction of the baths on the sea front. All these lobbies used similar means to apply pressure – public meetings, deputations, memorials, lobbying, using 'old boy' networks, complaining to the Local Government Board and so on – as will be seen again in the following chapters.

Building up the New Town;
Tidying up the Old

L ocal politics is only a process, the means to an end; the end product com-
prises the services, capital works, bye-laws etc., which emerge from the
political arena. This chapter examines the provision of works and services
undertaken to turn Bray into the new Victorian town, and to 'tidy up' the
urban fabric and traditional way of life, seen by the civic leaders as impediments
to progress. The Town Commissioners were not the sole players in the development process. Indeed, before their establishment, some services such as
planning and water supplies, which later became the preserve of the public
sector, were provided privately. Moreover many capital development proposals
were attempted by private enterprise with private money. Various aspects of
Bray's progress are now considered in turn.

EARLY DEVELOPMENTS

Reference has already been made to two early decisions, made elsewhere, which
left a lasting impact on Bray's development. By locating their workhouse at
Loughlinstown, three miles distant from Bray, Rathdown guardians, with
limited Bray representation, created a growth centre for medical services,
employment, and a range of suppliers, away from the town.[1] This stood to its
detriment for over a century, until improved transport reduced the disadvan-
tages of distance. Nevertheless, modern Bray with a population of 27,000, is
still uniquely lacking in hospital facilities. The decision of the railway company
to serve the town but to lay the track between the town and sea-front rather
than to the west of the built-up area as had also been considered, had a more
complex effect.[2] Its location is said locally to have resulted from pressure by
the earl of Meath not to have the line cross his estate when it would be
extended southwards from Bray, but to have it routed instead around the cliffs
of Bray Head. Neither the railway historian, Kevin Murray, nor the present
earl of Meath are aware of any written record of this pressure.[3] On the debit
side of this decision, the physical barrier of the railway limited the sea-front
area, and separated it from the town. More importantly, it cut off the town's
docks from the open sea, injuring trade and fishing, and eventually prompted
the building of a harbour on its seaward side. Had an opening span or a
higher-level bridge been provided across the river mouth and the river

dredged, a cheaper solution for the town's sea-borne trade requirements may well have been available. On the credit side, the railway opened the town to tourism and commuting traffic, though daily commuting took a considerable time to develop. It created employment both directly and indirectly by providing both goods and passenger facilities, thereby promoting the growth of trade and tourism, as well as attracting a wealthy residential population which brought money to the town.

Throughout the period, relations between the railway company and Town Commissioners were rarely amicable. They fought parliamentary battles over such matters as replacing the railway gates between town and sea-front with an over- or underbridge, and clashed over compulsory acquisition powers for the railway goods yard at Meath Road.[4] They fought a long legal battle over the rating of the railway: the Company secured a rating based on 25 per cent of valuation, against the 100 per cent sought by the Commissioners.[5] There were also clashes over pollution and fire danger from the railway's gas works, and over the seepage of water from railway underbridges onto public roads and footpaths beneath.[6]

Although the Commissioners would receive limited planning powers under public health legislation (covering matters such as construction materials and street building lines), early town planning in Bray fell to property owners who were involved in the drafting of leases. This resulted in an individuality of approach, the primacy of the owners' economic interests and general lack of co-ordination. Bray Commons Commissioners, also were engaged in the planning of the Commons area. While examples of private enterprise planning are seen throughout this work,[7] two case studies illustrate the process.

The first concerns the Donnellan estate which held considerable lease-hold property in both Big and Little Bray. When Captain Donnellan stated in court in 1853 that his family had been 'great benefactors to the town', he mentioned the free gift of the land for constructing Castle Street, and the widening of Main Street from thirty feet to sixty feet.[8] The wide new Castle Street, in effect a bye-pass for Little Bray, left the Donnellan estate with two valuable building frontages. The widening of Main Street, can only have affected the small section at St. Paul's where a small road island and a row of houses between the church and street were removed. Yet, these developments were of lasting benefit to Bray.

Again in 1858 an interesting, imaginative, small, private, urban renewal scheme was planned around St. Paul's Church of Ireland Church. It proposed the construction of Herbert Road as later built, with the extension of St. Paul's churchyard to the Main Street/Herbert Road corner through property clearance. It also envisaged clearing the houses below the church on Mill Lane and on Main Street opposite the Court House. It would have provided the town's most prominent site for a new or extended St. Paul's. Old lanes were to be closed. Church Terrace cottages were to lose their back yards, be turned 'back to front' to face the new (Herbert) road, and be given new yards at the rear.[9] Why was it never completed? In an internal rivalry between those Church members seeking the expansion of St. Paul's, and others favouring a new church near 'the Pound' (now the town hall), the latter prevailed with the opening of Christ Church in 1863.[10] The proposal may also have foundered on opposition from lessees in possession. In the event, only the new road was opened up, with Church Terrace cottages being cut off from their yards with no substitute provided, thereby creating one of the more insanitary areas in the town.[11] The abandonment of the scheme represented a major opportunity lost – for redeveloping St. Paul's Church, as the predominant feature of the town.

THE BOOM YEARS

K.M. Davies has described Bray as 'a town with a dual personality', the Victorian town and the old town.[12] This section deals solely with the Victorian development. The boom period in nineteenth century Bray lasted just a few years around 1860. The railway had arrived in 1854. Development of suburban houses and hotels expanded rapidly about 1858. The boom was waning by 1863. Virtually all the best Victorian development in Bray stems from this short period. There were the churches – Christ Church (1863), the Methodist church (post 1859), St. Andrew's Presbyterian church (1860). There were the terraces – Westbourne, Goldsmith, Prince of Wales, Dargan (now Duncairn), Florence (part), Brennan's, Brighton, Alexandra and Martello terraces, with Sydenham Villas and the south side of Quinsboro Road. Breslin's Royal Marine Hotel, built slightly earlier in 1855, (now replaced by Katie Gallagher's) and the International Hotel, which opened in 1862, (now site of the Bray Bowl), were the only large hotels (apart from the older Quin's Hotel) until the turn of the century. Bray Head Hotel opened about 1860, in what is now a small rear annex, and was gradually extended.[13]

The main impetus for this development came from a small group of property owners, financiers and contractors. John Quin the younger, received possession of his father's lands, stretching from the Main Street to the sea, in 1852. He sold the station area to the railway and assigned thirteen acres to William Dargan in 1858, including much of the site of Quinsboro Road, which became the town's premier shopping and residential area.[14] Other building leases followed with covenants to build to specified standards. One can see in these leases the landlord enforcing his own use zoning, density zoning and services provision, as a planning authority would today.[15] William Dargan is best known as the financier and developer of railways, canals, the Dublin Industrial Exhibition of 1853 and the National Gallery. But he took a personal hands-on interest in Bray after the railway arrived, providing capital, vision and energy. He built Duncairn Terrace, some of Quinsboro Road and the Turkish Baths. He laid out the Esplanade. He gave a lead which others followed.[16] One follower was Edward Breslin whose career has already been considered.[17] There was also James Brennan, a Bray man, who had made his fortune abroad and invested it in Brennan's Terrace and in the 250-roomed International Hotel.[18] There were many other smaller players such as Sidney Herbert, who laid out Herbert Road, and Sir William Wilde (Oscar's father), who built Esplanade Terrace during the boom period.[19]

The boom appears to have resulted from a fortuitous concurrence of a wide variety of factors. Firstly, there was the coincidence of landlords willing and able to give long unencumbered leases of development land under a policy of enforcing high standards, to men of wealth willing to invest in the town, and persons of vision and energy capable of using the capital creatively. Secondly, the railway was a multi-faceted facilitator – investing its own capital in the town, providing facilities for fast commuting and for tourism, promoting the town to the mutual benefit of its own and other interests, and having in its advertising system an efficient means for promoting the town. Thirdly, Bray's seaside location in Wicklow, 'the garden of Ireland', favoured the fashionable image of a health resort and scenic touring base. Fourthly, the ample supply of level, serviceable building land close to sea and town, favoured early development. Next the growth of population in Dublin and the social and political pressure to move from the inner city, provided a ready market for both permanent housing and seaside or summer homes.[20] Sixthly and finally, the tradition of wealthy Dubliners taking villas in the Bray area for the summer season, and of their using the regular pre-railway car services or commuting by private car, provided a firm foundation for development.[21]

Apart from making money, the primary objective of the coterie of Bray's developers has traditionally been seen as creating in Bray 'the Brighton of Ireland'. This appellation, widely used for a century, will be found, on examination, to have been merely a marketing ploy, a promotional gimmick, because the comparison – undeniable as an aspiration in some respects – was totally unrealistic in others. This was true even during the short period of Bray's frantic development. The earliest known printed use of the phrase 'the Brighton of Ireland' is found in April 1861 in a property advertisement. How realistic a comparison was it? In the year that Bray got its railway, Brighton became a borough. It already had a population of 70,000, and was in a different financial league. But Brighton, also a seaside resort and a commuter town, enjoyed the image of fashion, and exclusivity, which Bray hoped to replicate despite the absence of a major ingredient of Brighton's success – royal patronage.[22] It might be noted that the International Hotel in Bray was considerably bigger than Brighton's largest hotel, The Grand, opened in 1864.[23]

AFTER THE BOOM

Why did Bray's building boom come to an end? There appear to have been a number of interacting factors. No boom can last forever. There is evidence that targets were over-optimistic: the Turkish Baths lasted five years at most; the International Hotel closed and changed hands three times in the first six years.[24] There were external circumstances. While the railway opened up Bray in 1854, its two new suburban lines equally facilitated development of the rival coastal townships and the inland areas closer to the city. And the uncertainties of the Fenian period resulted in the collapse of other suburban building programmes such as 'Old Foxrock'.[25] But Bray's economic cycle of the early 1860s was almost the inverse of the national cycle, a phenomenon perhaps explained by Bray's once-off special inward flow of capital investment[26] – and this forces us to search for local solutions to explain the demise of the boom.

James Brennan died in 1862. William Dargan died in 1867. John Quin died in 1869. Brennan's son-in-law Charles Dufresne eventually resumed proprietorship of the International Hotel and his son John Brennan inherited house property, but neither of them was a developer: Dargan's personal interest in Bray died with him: Quin's successor, Matthew, carried out some development on Meath Road but died in 1877 aged thirty-six, leaving a young family.[27] Sidney Herbert died in 1861 and with him much of the family's interest in Bray. A later Lord Pembroke wrote to his agent 'I should like you to tell me . . . is any of the Rathdown union a part of my property . . .'.[28] And the Putland family, who owned most of the land south of Convent Avenue, from Newtown Vevay to the sea, lost Charles Putland in 1874 and his son George aged thirty-five in 1876. After this the property passed to an English branch of the family and remained tied up in family trusts until well into the twentieth century.[29] The replacement of the fortuitous assembly of developers by a group of passive landowners must be seen as the major reason for the slow-down in the town's development.

By 1870 the entire sea-front area was already built up, and there was some development west of the railway.[30] By 1900 only very limited additional infill of cheaper houses had taken place in the Victorian town mainly in the Meath Road, Adelaide Road and Florence Terrace areas. The first two of these were in small groups of houses of dissimilar design, indicating 'small builder' activity. And a cheaper speculative estate was by then in course of construction in the Seapoint Road area.[31] But in 1899 it was claimed that 'there were not three houses idle in Bray', a sure sign of an approaching period of building activity.

As to the nature of the new town, a letter to the *Bray Gazette* in 1866 referred to the absence of a year-round population. And various particles of evidence, such as a throwaway remark of Sir Charles Cameron at the 1876 commission of inquiry regarding his family's summers in Bray, or a letter in 1898 from the town clerk to the Local Government Board pointing to 'Bray families going to town for the Winter', point to the gradual growth only, of the year-round commuter.[32]

Before the railway came, Samuel Lewis had noted the availability of visitor accommodation in Bray.[33] Frances Seymour referred to 'the fashion of Bray gentlemen letting their places in the summer to Dublin people especially lawyers and judges'.[34] And the Ordnance Survey letters refer to the 'numerous bathing lodges rented out for the season to casual tenants'.[35] But there was a cycle of demand for summer accommodation. John Brennan had to reduce his rents for summer houses in 1866 due to previous over-optimism and the 'damaging effects of the Fenian conspiracy'. Yet this form of accommodation retained its importance throughout the period, and a list of visitors (not necessarily comprehensive) in July 1901, referred to 130 rented premises.[36]

Quin's Hotel, now the Royal Hotel, opened about 1770, and became one of the best known hotels in Ireland. With sixty bedrooms and extensive livery stables, it catered particularly, as has already been noted, for those devotees of the romantic movement with its interest in beautiful scenery, who flocked to Wicklow, and led Bray to describe itself as the 'Gateway to the garden of Ireland'.[37] The hopes of the 1860s, which added Breslin's and the International Hotel as competition for Quin's, were never realised. The International changed proprietors at least three times in the 1860s, at least once as a vacant premises, rather than as a going concern.[38] It was closed for periods, was sold again in 1875, was put up for sale in 1878 at £10,000 (half its building cost), but got no takers.[39] It was described in 1869 as rising 'phoenix-like' from the ashes of decay.[40] Most significantly, its rateable valuation, £455 in 1863, was reduced to £405 by 1870, £305 by 1881 and £260 by 1887.[41] A list of visitors to the town in August 1900 showed only forty-three guests staying in the International.[42] Breslin's Hotel stayed in one ownership till Breslin's death. But the valuation was reduced in 1877 from £300 to £150. The Bray Head Hotel, the third hotel of the boom years, had a valuation of £18 in 1869. This jumped to £60 by 1871, to £100 by 1875 and to £140 by 1887 due to extensions, but it went bankrupt and was sold by the courts in 1897.[43]

There was a handful of smaller hotels and boarding houses, the latter often run by women – widows – apparently part of the black economy and undocumented. A 1900 list of visitors mentions some twenty such premises but undoubtedly, given population statistics, the number was in fact much greater.[44] The 1901 census lists forty women and one man as 'Lodging House Keeper' – though this would include proprietors of both tourist accommodation and common lodging houses for transient workers.[45]

Bray had traditionally claimed a doubling of population in summer representing some 4,000 visitors in 1861, 7,000 in 1901. These figures, although unverifiable, seem exaggerated. There was a special local census in Bray on 6 September 1876, totalling 8,773 persons, implying a total of 2,500 visitors.[46] Bray's high season only ran from June to September with some residents spending seven or eight months in Bray while passing the winter months in the city.[47] On census day in April 1901 there were only eight guests in Breslin's Hotel, three in the International and one in the Royal.[48]

The railway's arrival boosted the 'excursionist' tourist market. There were excursions for events, excursions for 'communities of interest' – from firms, city districts, church groups etc. – excursions to coincide with Easter and Whit. In August 1855 there were cheap trips to Bray 'in lieu of Donnybrook Fair', which had recently been suppressed. 'Great crowds' were reported on fine week ends. On Whit Monday in 1894, 20,000 people were said to have visited Bray, and 1,200 pints of stout were sold by 7 p.m. in one restaurant alone. Cyclists appeared towards the end of the century: one reporter in 1901, counted 182 bicycles outside the Royal Hotel, and motorists were reported to have visited Bray in March 1901.[49]

Though the boom years around 1860 were never to be repeated, the town gradually evolved as a resort catering for a variety of visitors – a hotel clientèle, a two-residence community with city and suburban homes, short-term house renters, boarding house lodgers, and more down-market day trippers.

ESPLANADE AND PROMENADE

In 1859, William Dargan, realising that a seaside esplanade was essential for a seaside resort, leased the strip of ground between the Strand Road and the sea-shore from Lord Meath. It consisted of sand banks roughly contoured, and covered with marram grass, but Dargan had it fenced, levelled, and laid out as lawn.[50] He maintained it during his lifetime. The Commissioners then became responsible, a situation endorsed by the Township Act of 1866 which also authorised the extension of the esplanade south of the Cockbrook stream into the Putland estate. This extension took place in the 1880s but there remains a noticeably lower standard of design at this southern end.[51]

Maintenance of the esplanade deteriorated after Dargan's death and in 1869 Lord Meath threatened repossession on grounds of dilapidation.[52] As early as 1868 protective piling was provided because of erosion. Regular encroachment by the sea occurred during the 1870s.[53] When a protective sea wall was unanimously agreed in 1880, a decision was taken to incorporate an eighteen foot wide concrete and asphalt promenade similar to those in other seaside resorts. With parliamentary approval, the wall was completed by 1886.[54]

The esplanade and promenade became the venue for military band performances, 'white coon' and minstrel variety shows, regattas and other contemporary attractions.[55] But the Commissioners retained strict control.[56] Preaching, collecting money, riding of bicycles and tricycles, and roulette tables were banned to preserve the esplanade and promenade as a peaceful oasis for leisure and passive recreation of 'respectable' citizens, free from

unsolicited accosting or interference.[57] In 1889, a proposal for privately run
tennis courts was turned down.[58] Similarly in 1890, a switchback railway
proposal which Breslin said would make a 'Donnybrook Fair' of the esplanade
was rejected. It was argued that 'after a switchback railway had been erected
in Blackpool a class of person frequented the town, who from the noise they
created drove the better class of people away which was a great loss to the
town'.[59] Obviously the Commissioners still strove for the upmarket clientèle.

The increasing interest of Victorian tourists in flora, fauna and geology was
reflected by the opening in 1896, of the cliff walk to Greystones. Charles
Putland had allowed access to the summit of Bray Head as early as 1861.[60]

PROMENADE PIER

Like an esplanade, a promenade pier was indispensable to a Victorian seaside
resort. Piers became centres of fun, often providing in addition, berthing for
excursion steamers.[61] Many such proposals were prepared for Bray sea-front, the
first, a 300 yard iron pier or jetty for 'recreation of visitors and inhabitants' as well
as for commercial shipping, a notice for which appeared in the *Dublin Gazette* in
November 1863.[62] Others followed – of various lengths, facilities and locations
(five distinct proposed locations can be identified), often with bullish financial
projections and comparisons – 'Blackpool doubled its clientèle after its pier was
opened'.[63] One Commissioner proposed the purchase of a second-hand pier
from Douglas, Isle of Man. As can happen with an individual politician's kite-
flying proposal, it died when examined in the engineer's office.[64]

The most serious proposal was in 1896 for a combined tramway system
and a promenade pier. The tramway aspect was soon dropped. The usual
pattern was followed. A salesman arrived at the town hall proposing a pier
with an 800-seat hall, with facilities for excursion steamers to call. The
esplanade would be leased to the promoters, who would invest £40,000. Great
enthusiasm was shown by the company initially, but this was later replaced by
foot-dragging and giving of excuses for failure to commence such as 'the Boer
War' and 'great financial upset in London'.[65]

In 1998, as in 1857 Bray has no promenade pier. Despite the active support
of the Commissioners, the fluctuations in financial markets and perhaps the
fears of the Home Rule situation here, always tilted the risk/benefit ratio
beyond its limit for a town with so limited a tourist market.

BATHS AND BATHING; TOURIST FACILITIES

As appropriate to an aspiring health resort, Bray's first tourist facility – though
also its first failed investment – was the Turkish baths, constructed in the late

1850s, by Dargan, who was himself an enthusiastic client of such establish-
ments.[66] The building, of 'unequalled magnificence', was constructed of red
and white brick in Oriental style complete with minarets (shades of the Royal
Pavilion, Brighton!). It was opened in October 1859. Dr. Baxter, director of
St. Anne's hydropathic centre, Blarney, addressed the gentry of Bray on its
benefits.[67] The facility remained open for only a short time and, in January
1865, the Commissioners pledged every assistance to 'induce its reopening' by
Dr. Baxter, who by then was himself considering its purchase.[68] But this rescue
attempt failed; the baths hall itself became an assembly hall, with other parts
of the building being rented to religious sects and individual families. It
degenerated into a slum with clothes drying on the ornamental trees, fowl
scratching in the gardens and filthy insanitary conditions inside.[69] Another
'hydropathic establishment' based in Galtrim House adjacent to the baths, also
operated for a period around 1860.

Sea-bathing was of the essence for Victorian seaside resorts and, from an
early date Bray was equipped with bathing boxes.[70] Some were provided by
individuals; the railway company tendered for 'a range of bathing boxes' in
1857; the Loreto nuns had their own boxes. Work on 'extensive hot, cold and
sea-water baths' at Martello Terrace commenced in 1861 and served the public
into the twentieth century.[71] Victorians worried about the morality of
swimming attire and of dressing and undressing in public. They saw the need
for segregation of sexes on the beach, and Bray introduced bathing bye-laws
in line with such thinking. The 1870 revision allowed males to swim within
100 yards of the river, 'wearing drawers'. They could, of course, also swim away
from the Esplanade – on the 'back strand' or at the Cove. Females and boys
under ten, could bathe along the shore from opposite Quinsboro Road to the
Martello Tower (opposite to-day's Strand Hotel). A cordon sanitaire separated
gentlemen's and ladies' bathing areas, and boats and males were forbidden to
approach the ladies' area causing nuisance. Bathing machines were regulated.[72]
Yet morality was not preserved. 'Paterfamilias' complained to the *Freeman's
Journal* of men wearing short bathing dresses after 9 a.m. ('on Sundays
particularly') at the Cove where ladies passed by. One male resident objected
to swimming there because of the female presence. A young man was fined
for bathing near the ladies' baths at 10 p.m. one Sunday evening (for a bet)
when 500 people thronged the sea wall.[73]

Eventually a permanent Ladies' Baths was constructed. The Bray Pavilion
Company was launched in March 1878, its prospectus noting the 'deficiency
in provision for amusement and recreation of visitors' to Bray and proposing
to build 'a place of meeting' – a large saloon with promenades, refreshment
areas, reading and writing rooms together with a pleasure garden and Ladies'
Baths.[74] 415 shares were issued; 200 of these were taken up by Breslin, twenty
by Dufresne. Work commenced in April 1878 on a site on the esplanade,
leased from the Commissioners. Robert Henry Davis, a nearby resident, and

later a town Commissioner, sought an injunction to stop the construction, claiming interference with his view. A compromise was worked out; the baths would proceed, but the plans for the pavilion and pleasure gardens were shelved. The litigation destabilised the Company, which went into liquidation. Breslin lost his £1,000 investment, but bought out the baths and later sold them on to the Town Commissioners at cost (£825), plus legal fees.[75] A further Pavilion Company also involving Breslin and Dufresne, was founded in 1885, but foundered on the question of securing a site from the Commissioners on the esplanade. Their previous experience may have been a factor.[76]

The failure to complete the pavilion, like the failure with the promenade pier, was a major turning point in the town's development leaving it without any major wet-weather tourist facility. This deficiency thwarted efforts to promote the town right to the end of its days as a seaside resort in the 1960s, particularly after 'bed and breakfast' accommodation had become the norm.

One other major facility, Carlisle Grounds, was provided by Dargan in 1862, and was subsequently purchased by Breslin. It was leased for recreation – for athletics including professional challenges and gentlemen's races, for other activities such as cricket and archery, shows, skating, and fireworks. In 1885 it became so run-down that Breslin, as lessor, had to repossess it.[77]

The Bray Improvement Committee, was established in 1875 to overcome the lack of activities for visitors. It was renamed the Bray Amusements Committee in 1883. It organised events such as flower shows, band performances, fireworks displays etc. It raised funds and sponsorships to support these events, and promoted commercial tourist projects such as the pavilion, and the promenade pier. Its membership overlapped with that of the Commissioners – as would happen in any small town.[78] But, despite its efforts, Bray as a resort, always lacked adequate recreational facilities, particularly indoor facilities. This defect remained a disincentive to visitors and a detriment to tourism.

FLOODING AND EROSION

At the Royal Commission on Coastal Erosion in 1910, James McCormick, Chairman, Bray Urban District Council came under pressure trying to defend the council's formal submission which blamed 'parliamentary blunders' for Bray's major erosion and flooding problems, claiming that the town had spent £132,283. 15s. 9d. to date on remedial works. This figure was completely misleading, incorporating the cost of the promenade and harbour which provided other benefits in addition to coastal protection. Moreover it included both capital costs and revenue repayments on loans, thus counting certain costs twice.[79] It was an extraordinary submission to a public inquiry and bore all the hallmarks of a political decision being made (in this case, to seek government 'compensation') followed by an attempt to make the case fit the decision. The case was that, by approving the railway's plans prior to Bray having a corporate voice, parliament had subjected the town to damage by flooding and erosion.[80]

The Dargle River, short, fast-flowing and quickly surging after heavy rainfall, had before the railway came, a flood plain at Bray Commons and a wide valley opening to the sea. The railway embankment narrowed the mouth of the valley, while piling to support the piers of the bridge, restricted the river's depth.[81] The Bray Commons Commissioners and a private landowner built a retaining wall along the river's north bank in 1860.[82] The south bank was rising ground. Flooding of Little Bray occurred in 1867, 1882 and 1887 and disastrously in 1905 (when the flow was reinforced by the bursting of the 33 inch Vartry Water Main as the bridge which carried it across the Dargle was swept away). There is little doubt that an extra span at the railway bridge would have facilitated the flow, provided that Bray Bridge was also modified, the river's retaining walls set back, and the river upstream dredged. So the railway could reasonably disclaim responsibility. After further floods in 1965 there was major dredging upstream, but no proposal to widen the bridges.[83]

Coastal erosion at Bray only became an issue following development along the shore. In 1915 after a sixty year battle using groynes, piles, sea walls and rock armour, the railway company capitulated and abandoned 4.3 km. of track north of Bray, moving the line 400 metres inland.[84] Erosion was inherent in the unstable glacial till cliffs north of Bray. But removal of vast amounts of shingle from the beach by townspeople, by the Commissioners, and by the earl of Meath who drew shingle from both north and south of the river, aggravated the position. 14,000 tons were taken in one year; Lord Meath sometimes had twenty carts at work.[85] The railway company, fearing for their railway line, was in constant unsuccessful litigation to prevent these operations. Defects in the law and political support for shingle removal caused them continuous frustration.[86]

South of the river, the esplanade was breached as early as 1867, and protective piling and groins were constructed. But after further, almost annual damage, the sea wall/promenade was completed in 1886. This did not end the problem however; the wall was breached in 1941 and coastal protection works remain a matter of political controversy in Bray. Houses on sections of Strand Road were – and remain – liable to flooding when easterly gales coincide with spring tides.[87] The gas works with lime kilns and coal yard, were located on a very vulnerable sandy spit beside the river and were flooded a number of times. In 1872 due to flooding, the town was forced to fall back on paraffin lighting. This site was abandoned to the sea, and is now within the harbour area.[88]

Bray Head Hotel and the adjoining Fontenoy Terrace on the Strand Road, lost their access road, their pathway and their sewer, to the sea in the winter of 1874–5 forcing guests to climb a wall to reach the hotel. They remained without a road for a number of years as the Commissioners said it was private property. Eventually after legal and political friction a fifteen foot wide roadway with no path was provided. This was a short-sighted decision which still constrains the crowds approaching Bray Head from the promenade.[89]

In summary, it appears that the railway's construction cannot, despite the council's submission, be blamed for the erosion. But there is some evidence that the Commissioners themselves, by building the harbour in 1891–6, caused scouring i.e. washing away of sand, (which in 1896 uncovered the forest, just north of the harbour, which had been submerged some 5,000 years ago).[90] And many people must share in the blame for removal of shingle from the beach.

DOCK AND HARBOUR WORKS

Bray traditionally had a small sea-borne trade, importing coal, timber, slates and limestone.[91] The Seymour family, coal importers and merchants, had a small dock between the river mouth and Bray bridge. Other importers, Cuthberts and Cummings, discharged cargo on the river banks as a falling tide beached their small craft. Seven boats were Bray-owned in 1837, all of seventy tons or less. Alexander Nimmo, the well-known engineer, had proposed a pier for Bray but, like many similar subsequent proposals, nothing concrete emerged.[92]

The new railway bridge ended riverside docking, and forced boats to unload on the open beach – a dangerous operation with small sailing boats. Around 1860, the railway company constructed an alternative dock outside the railway as required by the Admiralty.[93] However no maintenance arrangements were put in place; no one assumed responsibility for it, and it soon lay abandoned, damaged by successive storms, and filled with sand and debris.[94]

Private efforts to open the port, by cutting the sand bar and driving piles to maintain a deep channel, ended in controversy as boats were frequently driven against the piles. These were eventually removed.[95] In 1861, Matthew O'Reilly Dease offered to invest £10,000 in harbour works if other 'gentlemen' also invested.[96] A number of harbour proposals (hybrids of commercial, passenger, fishing and promenade piers) emerged in the 1860s. The Town Commissioners opposed in parliament the cargo traffic aspects of one such scheme, apparently to maintain its status as the embryonic harbour authority.[97] The Bray Township Act 1866 gave the Commissioners responsibility for building two sheltering embankments beyond the river mouth. Some work was carried out but when they failed to secure a loan, the operations were suspended.[98]

In the late 1870s and early 1880s, the town's attention was diverted towards securing a fishing pier[99] but when these efforts failed, the harbour project was resurrected. Political pressure stemmed from the belief that directly importing coal for domestic and gas company usage would substantially reduce its price. It forced all prospective Commissioners to support the harbour plans.[100] With parliamentary approval, work on the harbour commenced in July 1891 with William James Doherty as contractor. Few construction projects avoid problems between contractor, consultant engineer, and clerk of works, but physical threats between contractor and clerk, and less dramatic complaints of the clerk of works exceeding his powers, marked the Bray Harbour construction.[101] Finally on 10 August 1897 the harbour was complete – seven acres in extent and costing just over £46,000 against the tender sum of £24,929. Continuous dredging of the berths alongside the pier kept the harbour open, though it was accessible to colliers and cargo ships only when they arrived at full tide. Most of its area was dry at low tide prompting a wag at the board of guardians to suggest it as 'a nice dry site for the Bray cemetery'.[102] Complaints were also made about dues payable – yet the harbour never paid its way and in 1910 a harbour rate of 11*d.* in £1 was being levied on ratepayers.[103]

With hindsight it was a bad investment. It ran at a loss. It failed to attract the hoped for excursion steamers delivering holiday-makers with spending money in their pockets. The cargo trade was essentially in coal, a seasonal import which failed to pay its way. J.E. McCormick in 1899, was accurate when he recalled 'before the harbour was built, nobody dared say a word against [it]. It is popular now to speak against it'. The big loss was the alternative benefits the expenditure could have secured.[104]

PUBLIC LIGHTING

Public lighting, a basic component of 'town improvement', was a priority of the first Commissioners, who initially erected a few dozen lamps lit by gas purchased from a local company.[105] The gasworks was built in 1858, its foundation stone containing a time capsule of information on Bray for the benefit of future generations. These were the premises shortly afterwards abandoned to the sea in favour of a new site.[106] The supply was marked by innumerable complaints about cost and quality of gas, from both domestic consumers and the Commissioners. There were also demands for extended hours of public lighting – to midnight for the arrival of the last train, all night at Market Square on market day, and 'late' for social events.[107]

The service was uneventful until 1891 when electric light was introduced following tenders for a public lighting contract based on gas *or* electricity. Bray had previous experience of electric light from 1886 when band performances on the esplanade were illuminated by electric lamps.[108] In July 1892 the new town illumination, produced from coal and water power, was 'un fait accompli'. By January 1894 however, Gordon and Company of London, the owners of the Bray Electric Light Company, approached the Commissioners to buy them out, thereby municipalising the service by becoming suppliers of electricity to the town. The Commissioners dragged their heels, but with parliamentary approval, were forced by circumstances to buy the company from the liquidator. They put in new machinery and built a new power station chimney, while resisting calls from house-holders for lower charges. There was increasing demand for electricity however, and the electricity works were extended in 1900.[109]

ROAD BUILDING AND MAINTENANCE

Roads are normally a significant municipal service in a growing town, yet nineteenth-century Bray had an unusually muted roads history. By the time Bray secured a local administration, the main roads – Castle Street, Main Street, Killarney Road, Vevay Road, and Sunnybank – were in place and Bray Bridge, had been widened and reconstructed by the grand jury in 1856. With large estates free of intersecting roads within the town, the Commissioners undertook little road building.[110] Bray Commons Commissioners were required to build a road along 'the River Side' across the Commons. The Commons ended 780 feet short of Bray Bridge leaving the Town Commissioners with the task of bridging the gap. It was recorded above how problems of title

2. Bray Bridge (1842)

delayed construction, and the road was not formally opened until 1873.[111] Reference has also been made to the private construction over green fields of Herbert Road and to the Commissioners reconstructing the southern end of Strand Road.[112] Later the urban district council used the Housing Acts to make a link between Florence Road and Main Street. In the main, however, the Commissioners' role with regard to new roads consisted of taking-in-charge private estate roads. The uncoordinated laying out of estates created anomalies to which the lack of alignment between Adelaide and Meath Roads, and the dangerous Novara Terrace/Novara Avenue Junction still testify. Had strategic road planning been recognised as a public authority function during Bray's period of fastest growth, much of the twentieth century's traffic problems could have been averted. Nevertheless Strand Road, Quinsboro Road, Putland Road, Meath Road and Sidmonton Road, though unimaginatively straight, act as major traffic distributors to this day.

From an early date the Commissioners undertook the flagging of footpaths, (often with a residents' contribution), and flagging of road crossings, three of which still exist. Maintenance work in the Victorian period consisted of unsophisticated surfacing in dry macadam.[113]

FIRE FIGHTING

As Bray expanded, the number of fire outbreaks increased – in houses and hotels, in the gas works and in hay ricks. Prior to 1870, fire fighting was ineffective with no 'fire corps' and no equipment. Neighbours, assisted by constabulary fought fires with buckets of water. In 1869 'a sub [police] inspector and head constable quickly marched a detachment of men to a blazing unoccupied house at Novara Road, only to find that the roof had fallen in'.[114] When Breslin's recently completed stables were gutted in October 1864 and the entire hotel was threatened, the Commissioners were criticised for lack of a fire service and 'not a drop of water'. Dublin Fire Brigade 'went down to Bray' in response to a telegraphed message but their two fire engines (pumps) proved useless without water.[115] As early as 1862, a fire engine for the town was suggested, but apparently was not provided until the new century, as purchase was again considered in 1900. While a city might aspire to horse-drawn steam pumps, the technology available to a small town was limited to hand pumps and hoses. Therefore much more valuable than a fire engine was the arrival of high pressure piped water in 1870, and the purchase of hoses which could be fitted to stand pipes.[116] However, the organisation to use such equipment was lacking, no hose being available when two houses were burnt in Little Bray in 1873, and no water being available at Allen's bakery fire in 1876.[117]

Not surprisingly the fire fighting arrangements came under scrutiny in the 1876 Commission of Inquiry. The fire brigade consisted of Frank Murray, the water inspector, and two carters normally engaged in scavenging who 'generally come to [Murray's] assistance'. Breslin acknowledged the danger of Murray alone knowing anything about the stop cocks (for turning up water pressure).[118] This lack of organisation was ironically illustrated when Murray's own thatched home went on fire in 1880. His neighbours saved most of the furniture and the constabulary attended, but by the time Murray was contacted, procured the hose and laid on a line, 'the fire had got full possession' and the house was gutted. In 1882 the hose was kept in the stores at the fair green, the key being retained in the constabulary barracks some hundreds of yards away. The Commissioners were pressing the R.I.C. to agree to hold the hose itself, instead of the key.[119] While the constabulary continued to participate in fighting fires into the new century, the system grew up of Commissioners' staff also turning out when the alarm was raised. As a bonus was paid for attendance at fires, the staff in effect had become professional fire fighters.[120]

PEOPLE'S PARK

Unlike the esplanade, the People's Park in Little Bray was rarely discussed by the Commissioners, was starved of funds and was never fully developed. The House of Lords Committee, when considering the 1859 Bray Commons Inclosure Bill, literally laughed at the proposal for provision of two or three acres (out of fifty-seven) as a public park to compensate the inhabitants for loss of recreation and exercise rights on the Commons. The Lords increased the allocation to ten acres.[121] It was envisaged that the Park's trustees, the Town Commissioners and Lord Meath, would receive the land duly fenced, and that it would be developed ex rates, or by selling off residual lands allocated to them under the Inclosure Act. In the event the lands were not sold off until 1880/1. When previously Sir George Hodson had offered money and shrubs for the park subject to the Commissioners providing a caretaker's lodge, the Commissioners were financially unable to respond.[122] Eventually in 1882 Lord Brabazon offered to build the lodge and implement basic development works, in return for an extra £10 per annum rent on the town hall/market house, this manoeuvre effectively being a loan of the necessary funds. While the park was never fully developed, it was at least available for football and passive recreation for the people of Little Bray.[123] The park was never a tourist facility, nor was it used by Big Bray residents – which perhaps explains the evidence of a witness at the 1876 Commission of Inquiry who affirmed that while hundreds of pounds had been spent on the Esplanade 'they have done nothing for the poor people'.[124] Financially the park was seen as an unsolicited burden on the ratepayers.

CIVIC SPACE

Bray has no town square. A monumental fountain locally dubbed 'the statue of the devil', (actually a Wyvern or winged dragon) occupies the civic space in front of the Town Hall. The fountain was first designed as a base for a knight in armour representing a Meath antecedent. But in 1882, during the period of popular ill-feeling against Lord Brabazon, his architect T.M. Deane suggested to Lord Brabazon the replacement of the knight with the Virgin 'who traditionally presided over fountains', to ensure respect for the work of art. 'I do not know whether you would think this was pandering to the R.C.s . . . we have as much right to the Virgin as they have'. There is no recorded response but subsequently the design incorporating the Wyvern, a Meath or Brabazon family heraldic design, was adopted.[125]

TIDYING UP THE OLD

The old ways and the established traditions sometimes impeded the 'improvements' planned for the town, and had to be addressed by the pacemakers.

BRAY COMMONS

The Commons, fifty-seven acres in extent, lay in two separate locations adjoining Little Bray. They were used by the public for grazing cattle, horses, asses, sheep and pigs, as a source of gravel and sand, for storing timber, for rights of way, by children playing 'common' (camain), for unloading boats, for drawing nets and landing 'sea rack' (seaweed). Bray Fair and Bray Races were held on the Commons and there was encroachment by squatters erecting cabins.[126]

In November 1858, the *Dublin Gazette* carried a formal notice of an Inclosure Bill to extinguish common rights, provide roads, allocate equitable portions to valid claimants and provide land for public exercise and recreation.[127] After three months the news leaked out to Bray, resulting in a protest meeting. There had been no consultation: notice was 'not in the papers read by us'. There were anti-enclosure speeches with emotive language 'it is too long ours to let him [Lord Meath] get it', 'Confiscation of Commons', 'land aggrandising parties', 'privileges of our fore-fathers', 'making the poor poorer and the rich richer'.[128] A motion in such terms was refused by the chairman P.W. Jackson, chairman of Commissioners, on a technicality, but he agreed to try to have the bill postponed and the people consulted. Interestingly those who called the meeting, the miller, a vintner and a wheelwright, were not exactly the most deprived; the squatters in their cabins remained on the margins. These were not notified of the proposal, they could not dream of lobbying in London and inhabitants *per se* had no *locus standi* there, even though they would be heard on sufferance.[129]

The proposals seemed reasonable – the Commissioners, a barrister and an engineer, would bring semi-derelict land into order and use, to the benefit of valid claimants of rights, and of the public generally. But there is evidence of hidden agendas: a plan to transfer Sidney Herbert's 'pauper tenants' from Big Bray to Little Bray; a desire by Dargan for the removal of the nuisance of loiterers – albeit on the far side of the river from his new estates; a demand by Lord Meath for the entire Lower Commons (fifteen acres) as his price for not opposing the Bill. Following amendments, including the major increase in park land from two or three acres to ten acres, and the reduction of Lord Meath's allocation (as lord of the manor) to one-sixteenth of total acreage, the Bill was enacted as the Bray Commons Inclosure Act 1859.[130] The Commissioners considered claims by squatters, allowing about thirty-five claims of smallholders proving possession in excess of twenty years. A few claims failed.[131]

The net result of the Commissioners' operations was that order was brought on the Commons, that squatters gained security – subject to scaled payments if they had less than twenty years of 'tenure', that a few persons proving grazing rights received small lots in compensation, that the town gained a fenced park, a fair green, a river wall, three watering places for animals, a stretch of roadway and some residual lots to produce future income, and that a large number of lots were sold to defray costs and to pay for the improvements. Despite the protestations of the objectors, despite the bad image of enclosures generally, it would appear that, assuming that public sales of surplus lots were at arms length – and they appear to have brought in unexpectedly high prices, thanks to soaring land prices generally in Bray – any loss of free access to the Commons in Bray, was more than balanced by benefits to the town.[132]

FAIR GREEN

Providing a fair green was a necessary step in bringing order to a rather undisciplined traditional activity. Lord Meath held the patent for fairs and markets in Bray since 1674, but tolls were no longer being collected from around 1840 because of opposition, even though the earl's steward could retain any monies he collected.[133] Around 1837 Bray had four frieze (cloth) fairs 'attended by all the Dublin dealers' each year and six 'cattle' fairs handling various kinds of animals. Evidence suggests an emphasis on trading rather than on social activity, though there were occasional reports of riotous behaviour. Evidence in one assault case referred to 'a show booth and tent' and 'show women'.[134] Mrs. Frances Seymour recalled 'booths [being] erected by the side of the roadway, in which the farmers could buy fairings [small presents] for their wives and children'.[135] The assault case evidence indicated that people gathered from 5 a.m. with business starting at 10 a.m. No clear demarcation of venue existed as various reports exist of activity on the lower commons, along Castle Street, on the bridge and at the old court house.[136] Some towns-people, who gave evidence to the Fairs and Markets Commission in 1852, commented on the public inconvenience of trading in the streets, and partic-ularly of slaughtering cattle on the footpaths, so the incorporation of a fair green in plans for the commons enclosure was not surprising.[137]

Although the Commons Inclosure Act became law in 1859, by the time the Commissioners had secured possession of the land, got bye-laws approved and rented out the tolls, it was not until January 1870 that the first fair was held in the fair green. Some extra-mural trading continued, but offenders were prosecuted whenever apprehended.[138]

MARKETS

The problem with markets paralleled that of fairs. Markets of agricultural produce were held in the Main Street on Tuesdays and Saturdays. There were no set trading rules, but business started at 3 a.m. or 4 a.m. to facilitate purchases being shipped to the Dublin market[139] and continued into the day, causing obstruction on the footpaths. Some shopkeepers caused analogous problems at all times, by trading from stalls outside their shops.[140]

The Commissioners wished to control hours and the location of trading. They publicly claimed that their market powers under the Township Act had superseded Lord Meaths' patent. They were publicly proved wrong. Breslin held that they had used the wrong approach – if they had sought a lease of Lord Meath's patent at a nominal charge, they would have got it. This was probably correct, because although Lord Meath forced the Commissioners to withdraw those provisions from their 1881 Bill which would have infringed his rights, he was prepared to rent them his patent rights in association with the new market house. This market house opened for business on 15 December 1884.[141] As in the case of fairs, the Commissioners encountered the problem of traders selling outside the market house. Producers, huxters and hawkers traded on the street or door-to-door, on non-market days when the tolls did not apply.[142]

CARMEN

Horse drawn cars for hire predated Bray's period of expansion and survived well into the twentieth century. The Town Commissioners gave high priority to regulating this service which was so important to the town. In 1861 there were already eighty-five car owners' licences issued (including thirteen dormant licences), a few owners having three, four or even five licences. One owner was a woman. Bye-laws were drafted as early as 1862 and licensing predated the Commissioners.[143] The 1901 Census lists 141 cabmen, carmen etc. in the town.[144] Controls restricted plying for hire to designated 'stands', they limited fares and they regulated conduct in areas such as furious driving, insolence to customers and refusing to take patients to hospital.[145]

Relationships between the carmen and others were often strained. At the 1876 Commission of Inquiry, no less than four witnesses complained of the carmen's conduct in terms like 'most objectionable . . . [of] filthy habits', 'disorderly conduct', 'celebrated and notorious for misconduct . . . heard of in Scotland and England', 'improper conduct . . . part of the history of Bray'. The report of the Commission in its short passage on Bray, referred to the 'almost universal extortion said to be practised by car drivers on visitors'.[146] The Town Commissioners were accused of over-leniency towards misconduct; cancelled licences were often restored by the politicians.[147] The nuisance inherent in car stands close to residences also caused contention, particularly at the upmarket Dargan (Duncairn) Terrace.[148]

The licensed carmen had their grievances too – against out-of-town carmen creaming off the holiday weekend traffic, against being moved from their stand at Dargan Terrace, against barrowmen being allowed to compete against them for business at the railway station.[149]

They had their own lobby, organising opposition to the banning of hired cars by Lord Powerscourt, from Powerscourt Demesne and 'the Dargle'. They regularly lobbied the Commissioners over their many grievances. On one occasion a month's notice of dismissal was given to the town's car inspector after complaints from a carmen's deputation.[150]

The carmen, unlike the commons, the fairs and the markets, were never fully controlled by the establishment, but their rights and the rights of passengers were at least held in a tense equilibrium throughout the period.

FISHERMEN

The development of the sea-front inevitably resulted in a clash of interests with existing users, most notably the fishermen. They had fished traditionally from the river mouth and near Bray Head, drawing their boats and drying their nets on grass banks, now forming the railway embankment, and the sand banks, now the Esplanade.[151]

The railway destroyed the river as a haven; the piling for the esplanade inhibited drawing of boats onto dry land. In 1870 the Commissioners lost a case for banning boats from the esplanade because of 'the prescriptive right of the fishermen to have them there'. They decided to provide a boat slip to avoid boats damaging the piling. In 1871 fishermen and supporters met outside Breslin's Hotel to protest against 'encroachments on public rights on the sea-shore'. They passed resolutions against 'illegal' enclosure of the esplanade, encroachment on fishermen's rights, spending of rates 'for [the] special benefit of one or two Commissioners' and neglect of the southern end of the shore (where most of the fishermen lived). But they strongly repudiated claims that they were opposed to progress.[152] The same year, James Lacy, proprietor of Bray Head Hotel and an owner of herring boats was prosecuted for trespass – drying nets on the esplanade railings. Lacy lost his case, and the Commissioners were awarded 6*d*. damages 'by agreement'. Breslin promised 'understanding' with regard to legal costs, and agreed to level a patch of ground for use of the fishermen. But, despite this compromise, the tension continued.[153]

In winter time there were storms causing damage to boats and loss of life. Martin Langton later recalled knowing 'fourteen young men belonging to the town whose lives were lost off the shore'.[154] The *Freeman's Journal* records numerous ship wrecks and loss of boats on Bray strand over the years.

In 1883 a high-powered committee including Lords Meath and Brabazon, Viscounts Monck and Powerscourt, was established to secure a fishing pier under the Sea Fisheries (Ireland) Act of that year. They sought to raise £2,000 for the 25 per cent local contribution required. Subscriptions were slow in coming in, so Breslin doubled his contribution to £50 and guaranteed any shortfall if £1,000 was raised, effectively underwriting the local contribution.[155] William Lane Joynt, D.L., solicitor to the treasury in Ireland and a Bray resident, pressed their case at the House of Commons special committee on harbour accommodation where he was opposed by Major Hayes, an Inspector of Fisheries who said 'I do not attribute much importance to [Bray]'. Later a procession of Bray fishermen and supporters carrying blue lights called to Lane Joynt's residence to thank him for his support.[156]

The climax of the campaign for a fishing pier coincided in January 1884 with the height of political tension over the town hall. Yet the committee held together despite allegations of fishermen being intimidated into supporting Lord Brabazon's position.[157] A public sworn inquiry was held on 11 January 1884. The court house was packed with Bray's religious and civic leaders, united in support, though barely on speaking terms with each other. William Lane Joynt appeared for the committee. A strong case was made for the pier, based on proximity of rich fishing grounds, a ready market for catches, the lack of any haven in sudden storms, the necessity for decked boats which were too heavy to be drawn up on beaches, and availability of local capital to arrest the decline in the local fishing and boat-building industries.[158] Forty-two fishermen and 335 dependants still relied on the fishing industry in 1880, according to *Freeman's Journal*, but the 1881 Census records only nineteen fishermen.[159]

Anticipation of a favourable response to the grant application was extremely high, particularly after a 'bullish' letter was received from Lane Joynt. But the secretary of the Fishery Piers Commission declined a grant for a pier because the fishing industry in Bray was 'of so unimportant a character'. He suggested a boat slip instead.[160] Senior public officials rarely use such tactless 'quotable quotes' and Lord Meath reacted predictably 'with astonishment and disappointment' in an open reply. In a further more conciliatory response, the Commissioners acknowledged the advantages of 'a harbour for goods and pleasure traffic' but pleaded lack of funds to support it. This was a valid point: the Piers and Harbours Act 1883 had provided the Commissioners with only £250,000 for harbour works. Having received 268 applications including Bray's, only the most urgent needs could be met. The Committee decided to fight on, but 'the day was lost' and the project was dropped.[161]

Thirteen years later the new harbour provided a safe haven for fishermen, but fishing never fully revived in Bray – although the 1901 census showed a small increase over 1881 to twenty-three fishermen in the town. Open boats continued fishing but in addition the boatmen adapted to the new milieu by hiring boats to tourists and bringing groups on pleasure trips.[162]

OTHER 'NON-CONFORMING USES'

There were other non-conforming users of the shore besides fishermen. Construction of the promenade in 1884 involved compensating local bathing box owners, one of whom claimed family ownership since his wife's great-grandmother's time. In addition, sand and gravel contractors drawing material from the beach were eventually forced to stop, and even seaweed harvesters were prosecuted.[163] To provide a modern streetscape facing the sea, some problems had to be addressed. The Bray Township Bill 1881 unsuccessfully sought powers to compulsorily acquire and clear one group of cottages between Breslin's Hotel and the sea. They were on the seaward side of the old track which was realigned as Strand Road. They were finally cleared around 1960.[164] More importantly, south of the Cockbrook stream, almost the entire sea-front area was occupied by dozens of small cabins on caretakers' agreements or at nominal rents, from the Putland family. Charles Putland sought counsel's advice on his rights for recovering possession but got little encouragement.[165] Consequently there is still a strong visual discrepancy between the fine villas and terraces from the Harbour to the Cockbrook, and the higgledy-piggledy disorganised sprawl, between the Strand and Bray Head Hotels. Here the status quo triumphed over Victorian 'progress'.

THE COMMISSIONERS' PRIORITIES

It is noticeable that the priorities of the Commissioners and the other developers, generally reflected the aspirations of the 'respectable classes' rather than those of the 'lower orders' who were generally without representation and without a voice. How the town fathers tackled working-class priorities such as slums are dealt with in the next chapter.

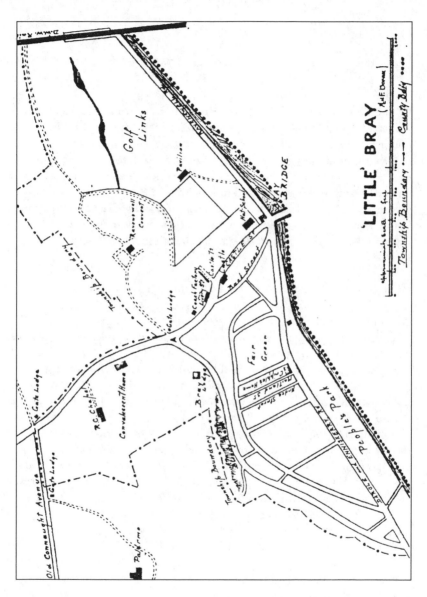

Map 3. Little Bray
From A.L. Doran, *Bray and environ* (Bray, 1903)

Public Health

The promoters of the 'Brighton of Ireland' as a fashionable seaside town, created considerable local prosperity. Yet many people lived in squalid housing conditions, lacking water and sanitation, and there is little evidence of the Commissioners giving priority to public health for the people. In 1865 a letter-writer to the *Freeman's Journal* complained that, while a quarter of a million pounds had been invested in buildings in Bray, 'nothing was done to remedy the crying evils of defective sewerage and an inefficient water supply'.[1] In this chapter, Bray's experience in providing sanitary services such as piped water and sewerage, and in tackling public health problems, is examined.

THE CONCEPT OF PUBLIC HEALTH

To understand the process locally, the general public health context must first be examined, for the demographic, economic, political, philosophical, medical and engineering developments of the nineteenth century, interacting on each other led to the evolution of the public health and sanitation concepts.

Public Health means the health of the community as a whole, and of its individual members.[2] The emphasis in the early Victorian period was on 'the sanitary idea', the removal of all 'miasma' – noxious vapours arising from filth – thought to be the cause of disease. Later the alternative more scientific germ theory, emerged predominant. However, the earlier 'miasmatic approach' though erroneous in theory was effective in practice for promoting public health.[3] The age of sanitation was 'the age of Chadwick'. Edwin Chadwick, a barrister, and a disciple and former secretary to Jeremy Bentham sought 'the greatest good for the greatest number.' In 1842 he produced a radical Sanitary Report.[4] Chadwick's strategy, all-embracing, centrally administered, uniform in approach, and with efficient direction of effort, was applied energetically to the removal of filth. House drainage, street drainage, water supply, street cleaning and paving were to be tackled together. However, it was only after his fall from power that this approach took legislative form with mandatory provisions.[5]

In 1854, Chadwick, was replaced on the General Board of Health by John Simon, a doctor who sought to develop a scientific base for sanitary law and administration, and who was responsible in the 1860s and 1870s for the first mandatory public health legislation. But most emphasis was still being placed on cleanliness and removal of nuisances.[6] After Simon in turn resigned in 1876, an era of preventive medicine arrived, and developments in epidemiology, confirming the germ theory, led to an individual rather than a communal approach to public health, with emphasis on notification of disease, isolation, disinfection, hospitals and ambulances, and a statistical basis for action.[7] It is worth noting that 'public health' later moved through a chemotherapy/'magic bullet'/ therapeutic approach, and, more recently, in a circle of events back towards environmental health, emphasising pollution, smoking, hygiene, diet – not too far removed from the Victorian concept of public health.[8]

The purpose of an administrative bureaucracy is to enable a central decision to be implemented in distant locations, situations and conditions, and Chadwick's, and Simon's influence can be clearly identified in the development of public health in Bray, indicating the effectiveness of the state bureaucracy. The Towns Improvement (Ireland) Act 1854 gave Town Commissioners certain *permissive* public health powers based on the concept of property owners themselves deciding how to spend their own money on communal services through the machinery of the local authority. The later legislation, particularly the Public Health (Ireland) Acts of 1874 and 1878 and the Local Government, (Ireland) Act 1871, which paralleled British legislation, drastically reduced local discretion in public health matters and transformed Town Commissioners into state agencies to implement each new development of policy in London.[9] The evolution of the various public health services in Bray is now examined.

WATER SUPPLIES

Communal water supplies were in existence long before the Victorian age: Roman cities had their aqueducts; thirteenth-century Dublin had an open conduit. But growth of industrial demand, the willingness of the upper-class to pay for pure water, and the advent of the water closet in the Victorian age, produced a social and engineering solution to the community's need for water, in the form of piped water supplies. Nevertheless for many, especially the poor, water supply in mid-century was still a primitive process.[10]

Knowledge of traditional water supply sources in Bray can be pieced together. Springs and wells have been found in the Lower Main Street area during reconstruction work at Winston's stores, the Royal Hotel and elsewhere, but hand pumps or buckets would have been needed to secure supplies.[11] No doubt, rain was also collected from roofs in water butts. In 1865, £30 was allowed by the Bray Commons Commissioners for 'providing a platform to reach pure water in the centre of Bray River beneath the bridge', from which is was drawn by 'carts and barrels'.[12] They also provided three access points to the river for watering animals.[13]

The small industries, the mill and brewery, were located beside the river from which they could draw abundant water for their own needs and Mr. Southern, the mill owner, provided a tank to 'sell on' his excess water to private owners and indeed to the Town Commissioners, for watering streets.[14] The first local reservoir (at Killarney Wood) and a piped water supply were constructed by the railway company after 1854 to water its locomotives, to meet its other needs for water, and the needs of the Turkish Baths. It also sold water 'to a few favoured residences'.[15] Initially, therefore, richer people in Bray could buy supplies from industrial firms or private contractors. Poorer people relied either on the few public pumps which tapped wells, or on the river and streams. Sinking pumps was an early activity of the Town Commissioners.[16] But this was only a palliative and the 'respectable' townspeople demanded plentiful supplies of water at adequate pressure.

The Dublin Corporation Act 1861 provided for damming the Vartry river at Roundwood, County Wicklow, and for supplying the coastal townships as well as the city.[17] Yet in 1864, while the Vartry system was already under construction, the Town Commissioners, in a spirit of enterprise or perhaps as a negotiating ploy, (or a bit of both) investigated the feasibility of securing their own supply. In the nineteenth century there were only three types of potential source: artesian wells (not possible at Bray), local rivers (considered precarious as regards continuity of supply in Bray) and upland catchment. A very suitable upland catchment area was identified near Enniskerry with granite base, dry weather flow, adequate rain basin, small area to be flooded for the reservoir, proximity to Bray, and adequate elevation. But Lord Powerscourt objected on the grounds of injury to game, to natural beauty and to fishing potential. So powerful was Lord Powerscourt that hunting and fishing got priority over drinking and washing, and the proposal was dropped without argument. An alternative site at Kilmurray, Kilmacanogue, eight kilometres from Bray, was identified and pronounced adequate for the town's needs in 1864.[18]

Two months later in January 1865, the Commissioners met Dublin Corporation Waterworks Committee under its chairman, Sir John Gray, to discuss Vartry supplies (i.e. supplies from the Roundwood reservoir) and the terms for such supply. The Corporation would supply in bulk to the Commissioners who could lay their own pipe network to supply 'for home, for fire, for street and all other private and public purposes'. Alternatively, the Corporation would supply individual customers as a water supply company. They would not discuss cost however, until the type of supply required was known. The Commissioners then referred to their alternative Kilmurray scheme. This did not appear to impress the Waterworks Committee who suggested that they estimate the cost of an enabling act, a reservoir, purchase of water rights, cost of pipes and other expenses compared with the cost of contracting for Vartry Water. They also queried the continuity of the Kilmurray supply.[19] Perhaps the Bray Commissioners were bluffing. They must have been aware of the heartache Dublin Corporation had suffered for many years, trying to secure enabling legislation while fighting off vested interests. They would have realised the responsibility of owning a reservoir, as the Dale Dyke reservoir disaster had occurred at Sheffield less than a year previously.

In the event, the Bray Township Act, passed in 1866, provided Bray with a high pressure water supply from the Corporation, at a rate of twenty gallons per person per day and at a cost of 4*d*. in the £1 on total valuation. Breslin, however, was still pressing for an independent supply in 1867.[20] By spring 1868 mains were being laid to carry the Vartry water. In October of that year plans for providing communal supplies (fountains) in poorer areas were drawn up. Vartry water flowed in Bray from June 1870.[21]

A series of legal disputes followed, lasting nearly thirty years. The statutory payments from the various townships were so low that Dublin Corporation was suffering a substantial annual loss. In 1874 a charge for water used in excess of the previous statutory allocation was imposed. But loopholes were found in the new legislation. No calculation of population was prescribed, so the chargeable excess, based on population, could not be determined. This loophole was closed in 1885. Then it was pleaded that excess charges were only enforceable where formal requests for an excess supply was made. Bray and other townships withdrew their existing requests but continued to draw excess supplies. This resulted in bad relations, reductions in pressure, demands for better pressure, demands that wasting of water be stopped, threats by the local townships to provide their own water, and so on. The loophole was finally plugged in 1897.[22]

A detailed assessment of the situation with regard to Bray's water supply can be made from evidence given at the 1876 Commission of Inquiry. People were asked to pay 5*s*. for a connection, a fee which many people could not afford. The water was therefore supplied free to poorer areas, by means of public fountains which were often some distance from the houses. Moreover some areas had not yet been served by mains. Only one man, the water inspector, knew how to balance the pressure between different parts of town.[23] Dr. Thomas Lowe Whistler, the dispensary doctor and sanitary officer, caused a controversy when he admitted drawing water from a well in the garden of his terraced house on Quinsboro Road rather than using the piped supply.[24] Dr. Whistler, Henry Brett, town surveyor, and Col. Henry Meagher a 'resident ratepayer', all alluded to the great scarcity of Vartry water in Summer 1876.[25]

Such complaints persisted, especially in drought years such as 1893, when the Corporation cut off supplies at night as a conservation measure, and offered assistance in tracking down waste water. But the Commissioners were only concerned with the shortfall in the town and not with the overall position.[26]

Given the Town Commissioners' experience with capital works, they would appear to have been fortunate in securing their supply of wholesome water on such beneficial terms from Dublin Corporation. While engineers

claimed that there was no scientific method for allocating costs to the townships for a share of Dublin's water supply, it appears that Bray's water was being
heavily subsidised by Dublin City ratepayers, at least up to 1897. Bray was
paying 4*d*. in the £1 on valuation (with additional distribution costs of 2*d*. or
3*d*.), while City ratepayers were being charged water rates totalling 1*s*. 3*d*. in
the £1 up to the late 1880s, after which they began to fall.[27]

SEWERS

The 'sanitary idea' implied immediate removal of all filth and ordure.
Traditionally, domestic solid waste – human and animal excrement and
household refuse – was considered a single product. Most dwellings, urban as
well as rural, had no disposal arrangements. Some families had dry closets
emptied occasionally to a communal ash pit, where dry refuse was added. Poor
families had little domestic refuse. Much filth was dumped on the street where
horse manure also accumulated. Farmers purchased accumulated waste as
fertiliser, providing income for some urban dwellers. 'It was removed in the
return country carts which had brought in vegetables and produce'.[28]

Liquid waste soaked away to cesspools, or alternatively polluted springs, wells
and streams. The introduction of the water closet, however, revolutionised waste
disposal, overwhelming cesspools, polluting street sewers designed for surface
water only, and discharging directly into streams, a hitherto illegal practice.[29]
Chadwick, despairing of utilising town sewage as agricultural fertiliser, em-
braced this 'policy of sewage' but promoted a system of drainage, separate from
surface water, in small sealed scientifically designed earthenware pipes, discharging away from built up areas. Paris and Berlin, by comparison, designed
huge sewers to take everything from surface water to industrial waste.
Chadwick's system eventually prevailed.[30]

There is some evidence of the existence of private sewers in Bray before
the new Commissioners took action. An 1860 lease required construction of
a box sewer measuring three feet by two feet, to serve both a new development and adjoining building land. The new International Hotel boasted
bathrooms and water closets, implying piped drainage.[31] The town's minimal
industrial effluent was discharged into the river.

On the day the Township Act came into force in 1866, giving extra spending
power, the Commissioners established a Sewerage Committee and considered
major sewerage works including a half mile main from Old Connaught to the
river incorporating 'sixty-three yards of open drain'. Plans for other sewers
followed, but evidence points to individual district systems, each discharging
to the sea front or the Dargle river rather than through a unified system. This
was normal practice at the time. Even the renowned sanitarian, Sir Charles
Cameron, defended sewerage outfalls to the Liffey as late as 1885.[32]

The Commissioners' efforts met a series of obstacles. An early priority was draining the cesspool from Hudson's Cottages near Novara, home of P.W. Jackson, Commissioner. Two options were available: east to the sea or north via existing sewers by Eglinton Road and Westbourne Terrace to the river. In each case, intervening owners objected, resulting in three years of indecision and lack of action.[33] At a macro level, finance was an obstacle. Delays in securing loan facilities twice caused suspension of sewer works.[34]

An interesting decision was made in November 1869 to defer making sewers in Little Bray and Newtown Vevay 'the effect of [proceeding] being to keep the rates for a few years too high to the detriment of the present interest in the township'. To attract investors and new residents to the town, the Commissioners had to strike a balance between providing attractive services and keeping rates low. Their solution here was to penalise the poorer areas – but the decision was reversed the following year.[35]

Legal difficulties also arose and objections were raised, not merely against specific way-leaves or outfalls, but against the principle of financing sewers by taxation. There were four possible sources for financing sewers, – the township rate, a sewer rate levied on a benefiting district, contributions from individual beneficiaries, and borrowing. The first and last represented a pooling of costs and a charge on all ratepayers. The second and third represented a whole or partial charge against beneficiaries. Quin, a property owner, objected to a sewer 'of no public utility [which] could not be charged against rateable property'. Thomas Johnson, a solicitor and non-resident ratepayer, objected that as his own land was drained by a private sewer to the sea, he was paying rates to subsidise sewers for other people.[36] The Commissioners' dilemma is a classic example of the ideological question of whether to finance social utilities by redistributing wealth or by directly charging beneficiaries.[37]

A committee was established to consider raising separate sewer rates. They got legal advice. They declared themselves a sewer authority under the Sanitary Act 1866. Eight districts were formed but the practical difficulties of apportioning expenses equitably among them were insurmountable, and the Commissioners decided to finance sewers by borrowing, though still seeking contributions from landowners in special cases.[38] This complied with the letter, though not the spirit, of the law because borrowing, like the township rate, was a town-at-large chargeability – a point not lost on Johnson who held that, being inequitable, as he saw it, it should also be illegal.[39]

Sewerage generally was a topic at the 1876 Commission of Inquiry. Edward Dempsey, town clerk, stated that the existing sewerage was good but a large portion of the town lacked it. And not all houses in areas already drained were connected. Some owners had to be summoned before they connected to the public sewers. Henry Brett, town surveyor said £3,000 had been spent on sewers; an equal amount was still needed.[40] But there were many defects. Dr. Whistler, the sanitary officer, accepted that Herbert Road sewer discharged into the mill race just above the brewery's intake 'injurious to the malting process' with the 'effect . . . on the malt . . . observed in Dublin'. Mr. Ussher, brewery manager, attended the inquiry to controvert such adverse comment on the brew, but conceded that he himself did not drink the water from the mill race. This complaint had been outstanding for over a year.[41]

From 1876 on, sewerage was no longer a matter for contention at the board; indeed it was rarely discussed. Isolated areas were connected to the sewers and interceptor sewers were installed to reduce pollution. The sea front interceptor, designed to intercept outflow from private and public drains which had previously discharged along the strand, and to carry it to the harbour area, was under construction at the end of the period studied.[42] In 1901 some 'rubble built' rather than earthenware sewers still survived in older areas such as Main Street and Castle Street. These resulted in water pollution, the escape of sewer gas and rat-carried disease. But all houses 'except poorer classes' had drain connections and the sewerage network was generally in place.[43]

CLEANSING

Evolution of cleansing as the third engineering-based sanitary service took place in Bray mainly in the twentieth century. But modern cleansing (street sweeping and refuse collection, recycling and disposal) had its nineteenth century counterpart in the freelance scavengers, who collected waste from privies and ash pits, from heaps and road scrapings, storing it before they disposed of it to farmers, or else dumping it under cover of darkness.[44] Poor people discarded little refuse.

The first Bray references to public scavenging related to street cleaning contracts and an 1870 decision to provide sites at the esplanade and west of the town, for storage of 'road stuff' 'until fit for top dressing'.[45] Scavenging was a minor topic at the 1876 Commission of Inquiry. The Commissioners employed poor quality scavenging staff to scrape the streets as part of road maintenance. Edward Breslin complained 'the scraping of streets by shovels and gathering in heaps the refuse and leaving them to rot and ferment is not what should be allowed'.[46] Dumping occurred 'in front of the Church' and 'everything is pitched into the river' for want of alternatives. One witness stated 'I frequently saw heaps of rotten straw, cabbage leaves and manure lying both in the Main Street and Westbourne Terrace' (at the town centre).[47]

Eleven years later, conditions had scarcely improved. In September 1887, the earl of Meath wrote to the Commissioners

> there is no person appointed by the commissioners to remove the accumulations of ashes, manure from closets, decaying vegetable, and other insanitary matter, as is done by the officials of Dublin Corporation.

These accumulations are left in Bray for the poor people to remove and the result is that many are unable or unwilling to incur the expense of carting away these unwholesome heaps of rubbish which remain far too long in their back yards to the great danger of their own health and that of their neighbours.[48]

Reporting on this, Comber, the town engineer, recommended cleansing of yards and ash pits monthly, April to September, and every two months in winter, for £1,200 per year. Kingstown already had such a service.[49]

Apparently nothing was done however because in February 1894, the desirability of providing a domestic scavenging service was agreed by the Commissioners as 'urban sanitary authority' and the overseer was instructed to 'remove dustbins for any residents who provide them'. At least one rate-payer objected to the charge of 1s. per week for a daily collection. Tenders for a covered dust cart were sought in Aug. 1900.[50] At the end of the period, ash bins were being collected twice weekly; while ash pits, often overflowing, were emptied at irregular intervals. The town employed two superintendents with fourteen men on domestic scavenging, and thirty-six on road cleansing. There was no tiphead in the modern sense but the two refuse storage depots provided in 1870 were now being termed 'objectionable'. This was progress.

HOUSING

In 1837 Samuel Lewis recorded 450 houses in Big Bray – 'one long street of irregularly built houses' and 230 houses and cottages in Little Bray.[51] But con-temporary Ordnance Survey Sheets show a classic phenomenon for a growing Victorian town – growth of infill courtyards and laneways at the rear of many houses, shops and inns along the street, implying local ownership, low cost housing and lack of living space. There is evidence of indiscriminate develop-ment by squatters on Bray Commons and by fishermen on the sea-front.[52]

Living conditions in Bray were discussed at the Bray Commons Inclosure Bill enquiry in 1859, with allegations, supported by the County Surveyor, that Sidney Herbert, son of the earl of Pembroke, with other landowners, had initiated the Bill so as to provide land for resettling 'the pauper tenants and weekly tenants in Great [Big] Bray on Little Bray', and away from their homes and developments.[53] The inquiry heard of 120 cabins in Great Bray with over 100 squatters. 'A very wretched description of squatter' dwelt on the commons. 'When they have built a cabin and made a little bit of garden they go on taking more year after year'. Chairman of the Town Commissioners, P.W. Jackson, asserted the need in Bray for the 'class of cottage suitable for the poorer part of the population'.[54] Thirty-five cottiers successfully claimed squatters' rights under the Inclosure Act. Two with wooden huts (one bought for £3 11s. 0d.)

secured alternative sites only after attending the public sale of commons lots, to protest their claim.[55]

Early Victorian public health reformers had targeted unhealthy dwellings for attention; Edwin Chadwick's comprehensive city-wide approach however, won the day in the 1840s and 1850s thereby delaying the tackling of the slum problem per se.[56] However, the Sanitation Act 1866 (for Britain and Ireland) extended the definition of 'nuisance' to include a house, and made action compulsory rather than permissive.[57] Or so it was hoped; in practice 'it combined ineffectuality in practice with revolution in principle'.[58]

Since May 1859, Bray had a nuisance inspector working from his home, 3 Church Terrace – a great irony showing the Commissioner's powerlessness to act – as the construction of Herbert Road in the 1860s left these houses without yard, ash pit or privy.[59] All filth was carried through the houses and dumped in the street. Later, Dr. Whistler wanted a rear access provided onto the new road but was told 'Lord Pembroke would not allow it' a statement which, admittedly, he doubted.[60] Difficulties in tackling nuisances were compounded by the Commissioners' 'do nothing' attitudes. In October 1870, a reported nuisance was minuted, 'Commissioners are only a Board to manage the affairs of the township and have no powers [untrue] to abate nuisances. A personal action can be taken'. Searches through newspapers and samples of minutes produce no evidence of tackling nuisances till after 1874.[61]

The Public Health (Ireland) Act 1874 established a comprehensive system of urban and rural sanitary authorities with defined duties. Bray Commissioners held their first meeting as urban sanitary authority on 5 October 1874. Immediately the town's 'black spots' were noted – Hudson's Terrace, Doyle's Field, Purcell's Field, Pound Lane, Mill Lane, Hall's Lane off the Main Street; Clifton's Lane, Plunkett's Yard, Back Street, Matthew's Lane, Dillon's Lane in Little Bray; isolated spots such as Chapel Lane on the Dublin Road, Newtown Vevay and the strand near Bray Head. But problems were found outside the lanes and courts: Reverend Scott's cesspit overflowed across the public road for many months; 1 and 2 Goldsmith Terrace caused trouble for over a year; the Assembly Rooms were a perennial problem. Breslin, the Town Commissioner, received a notice about conditions at Dock Terrace which he owned.[62]

The case of Goldsmith Terrace illustrates the practical difficulties of abating nuisances. In this three storey terrace of shops and dwellings, Arthur Doran, pharmacist, amateur historian, and future Commissioner owned No. 1; James Murphy, milliner and Commissioner owned No. 2. A shared defective w.c. cistern for long affected both buildings. Notices were ignored; court action produced no results; the Local Government Board was lobbied by the owners; three J.P.'s suggested 'a review' of the case to the town clerk; the sanitary officer was 'grossly insulted for daring to go into the house'; he was threatened with legal action if injury by loss of tenants resulted. Finally, in a second court case, the obstructing owner, Murphy, though claiming immunity because the condition was sixteen years in existence (i.e. predating the legislation), was given a continuing fine of 6*d*. per day retrospective for seven months. The nuisance was then abated.[63] Less dramatic was the conflict with Rev. J.G. Scott. He saw the need for a public sewer to Church Road; the Commissioners wanted him to stem the overflow from his cesspool. Finally after threats on one side and lobbying on the other, the sewer was laid by the Commissioners.[64]

In October 1876, Edward Breslin commenced a term as Chairman of the Commissioners with a tour of inspection and a report on improvements needed.[65] He could not anticipate the drama of 18 November 1876 – the opening day of the Bray hearing of the 1876 Royal Commission of Inquiry.

Edward Dempsey, town clerk, had concluded his opening evidence, having affirmed, inter alia, that sanitary conditions in Bray were 'in a very fair condition except [for] Little Bray'.[66] Then Dr. Thomas Lowe Whistler, dispensary doctor and sanitary officer, took the stand. Conditions were 'very unsatisfactory, indeed most unsatisfactory'. Some houses in all parts of town were 'unfit for human beings to live in – no yards, no ventilation of any kind, very little light, no water supply, no sewerage, they were nothing but dens'.[67] He gave examples from different parts of the town. On the esplanade 'her window looks out on a place where immediately under her, there is a most abominable privy, three dustbins and a pig sty'; at Railway Lane 'a woman ill . . . water five or six inches high [on the floor] . . . could not go in . . . last February . . . existing still'; in Purcell's field 'filthy manure brought out from a house to be removed . . . there for five days . . . when they begin to stir it, a fearful stench arises . . . field inhabited by 100 people'; Clifton's Lane 'an abominable place . . . the most wretched place I have ever seen. It is more that I can conceive how people live there'.[68]

His description of the town administration caused extreme problems for the Commissioners. Very few of his 179 Reports since 1874, concerning over 500 dwellings, had been dealt with. He had consulted the Local Government Board which confirmed he had satisfactorily discharged his own personal responsibility by reporting. The Commissioners met only monthly, and then only if there was a quorum, and, for example, there was no quorum in January or February 1875. Typically a month was lost before reports were considered. He could not take any initiative unless asked. When he tried to get lanes and back premises tackled, 'I am always told they are not under the rates' – a deliberate or unintentional misrepresentation by the Commissioners of their powers.[69] Various indicators exist of the Commissioner's low priority for tackling poor housing conditions: the lack of action on Dr. Whistler's reports, the lack of quorums at meetings, the lack of full time sanitary staff – the sub-sanitary officer was also the car inspector, nuisance inspector and lodging house inspector – failing to consult the external consultant sanitary officer, and the low pay of sanitary officers.[70]

Breslin reacted vehemently at a special meeting of Commissioners to Dr. Whistler's 'blowing the whistle'. He attacked him, using phrases like 'not the least foundation', 'his statements contradicted themselves', 'made for the purpose of getting an increase in salary', 'wild statements'. Breslin promised a repudiation at next inquiry session. He called in the eminent sanitarian Dr. (later Sir) Charles Cameron to tour Bray with him. He told Dr. Whistler not to come. But when Cameron gave evidence at the enquiry, he fully corroborated what Dr. Whistler had said.[71]

Breslin had expressed surprise and anger during the tour with Sir Charles. Typically, at the next session of the inquiry, he tried to blame others. He blamed the Commissioners 'I do not think [it was ever intended] to have such a class of men on the board'. He blamed the staff 'the poor old men are not able to work . . . [and should be replaced]'. He even blamed his own tenants of Dock Terrace where there were currently no privies and where, in one case, excrement was emptied through a hole in the wall 'I signed summonses against the parties living in that very place'. He submitted his recent report to the Town Commissioners, setting out various criticisms of the Board.[72]

Why did Dr. Whistler go public? His grievance over salary? Seeking publicity? Was he a dedicated official frustrated by the Boards' lack of understanding and commitment? He had previously sought and got assurances from the Local Government Board that he had discharged his responsibility by reporting to the Commissioners; his evidence was corroborated; Breslin's reaction showed lack of appreciation of the serious situation. Frustration appears therefore to be the most likely explanation. Dr. Whistler could have sued Breslin for slander. Instead he published a letter challenging Breslin's allegations 'as a professional man and a gentleman', while restating his case and declaring his altruistic motives. He got no response.[73]

In 1878, as part of Lord Brabazon's campaign to close off access to Ravenswell Road and his adjoining lands, he offered to build a 'public privy' to replace the use of his land by those residents of Little Bray who were without sanitary facilities – subject to the Commissioners maintaining and regulating it. He suggested that sale of manure could be a source of profit. There is no evidence of the offer being taken up.[74]

There is no evidence of a blitz on private substandard accommodation either before or after the 1876 Commission of Inquiry, but rather a long war of attrition. A recommendation of Dr. Whistler to close houses was, with the assent of the Local Government Board, not acted upon; neither were a number of 'wretched tumble-down cabins demolished as ordered by magistrates'.[75]

Sir Charles Cameron held that closing unfit housing was a cheap, effective solution for dealing with slum areas.[76] But in Bray they sought improvements rather than closing, indicating unwillingness to offend landlords or reluctance to reduce housing stock – or both.[77] In 1874 Dr. Whistler had recommended closure of fifteen houses at Hudson's Court containing fifty persons 'with neither sewers, water or ventilation'. They would have been reluctant to evict so many families at one time.[78]

A third potential approach to slum clearance, was the building of good quality housing thereby increasing supply and reducing the demand for the worst accommodation. In the 1880s Lord Brabazon built artisans' dwellings in Little Bray – Dargan Street, Maitland Street and Ardee Street. It was a business venture. He planned to build at £300 per unit to secure £30 per annum rent – a 10 per cent return – but was advised to build a bigger house for a higher rent. First dwellings were hard to let; his employee, Christopher Gannon advised, 'the rent . . . is too high . . . for [those] . . . that mostly live about Little Bray . . . it is quite easy to rent the [cheaper] cottages at Ravenswell Row'. In 1887 Dublin Artizans Dwelling Company, in which the Brabazons had invested £40,000, bought building lots from Lord Meath. And Fane Vernon, Lord Pembroke's agent, replaced 'unsightly and ruinous cottages by handsome and comfortable buildings' in the Kilmantain area in 1877.[79]

These schemes were not only commercial in orientation but selective with regard to tenants, as are most private housing associations from Octavia Hill's day to the present.[80] Without the local authority as the 'landlord of last resort' the poorest citizens were left to fend for themselves.

In 1885 the Royal Commission on Housing of the Working Classes (U.K.– wide) reported that failure to act, rather than defects in existing legislation, was the cause of lack of progress on public housing in Ireland.[81] Certainly, Bray built no houses until the urban district council was formed in 1899, but they could at least plead major involvement of commercial housing interests, and there were procedural defects in legislation, remedied in the Housing of the Working Classes Act 1890. This Act provided powers inter alia for dealing with unhealthy areas, unhealthy houses and house-building programmes.[82]

Building new dwellings on a 'green field' site before closing of unfit premises was discussed by Bray Commissioners as early as 1894[83] but without result. The new district council, within its first year, produced a slum clearance scheme and proposals for land acquisition for public housing. There was some opposition from nearby traders and householders adjoining the proposed Purcell's field scheme; there was some opposition from ratepayers fearing increased rate burdens. But opposition was muted and, after a public enquiry was held, a provisional order was confirmed in July 1900 authorising slum clearance areas in Little Bray, and purchase of land (including houses) for local authority housing and for opening up of roads.[84] These proposals were implemented outside our period of study.

Common lodging houses were premises where people lodged by the night or short period. They did *not* include – as widely believed in Bray – hotels or middle-class lodgings. They catered mainly for migrant men,[85] who followed construction work from place to place, hiring lodgings by the week or even by the night. They also housed new arrivals from the countryside seeking short-term shelter. A high proportion of migrant women, particularly in Bray, secured domestic work inclusive of accommodation. There is evidence that, during the construction boom around 1860, with the construction of the railway, the Vartry water system, housing and new hotels, the male population of Little Bray swelled with limited increase in housing accommodation.[86]

The Commissioners had powers to regulate such houses and they produced draft bye-laws in 1867. Only limited practical action was apparently taken however, though the Commissioners were aware of much overcrowding, more lodgers than beds, and poor sanitary arrangements.[87] In 1876 Breslin wrote to the Commissioners criticising non-pursuit of controlling orders. At the 1876 Commission of Inquiry, Dr. Whistler did not know how many lodging houses were registered or how many persons were accommodated. They were 'a pest' and some were condemned. Dr. Cameron heard some owners had been required to halve the number of beds following inspection.[88]

Neither is there much evidence of activity in later years. While in 1893 a report, following an inspection, claimed that the registered lodging houses were in good repair, it appears that in June 1900 only two lodging houses in Little Bray were registered, out of a reputed thirty, and the inspector said he had only power to inspect premises between 9 a.m. and 4 p.m. (when there would be no lodgers!) At the housing enquiry in March 1900, Bishop Donnelly commented that many common lodging houses were unregistered, resulting in 'promiscuity of sexes' and no safeguards for morality. The few references to common lodging houses in the minutes of the Commissioners 'as urban sanitary authority', confirms the impression that they were merely 'going through the motions' with regards to exercising their control.[89]

It is worth noting how the local authority housing service grew out of the concept of public health, via the application of public health nuisance legislation to dwellings, and the subsequent clearance of unfit houses and unhealthy areas. Specifically, with regard to Bray, the commercial housing sector provided all the working class housing accommodation until the urban district council built their first housing schemes in the new century.

PUBLIC HEALTH – GENERALLY

With the primitive hospital and medical administration for north Wicklow based at Loughlinstown workhouse, Bray had little responsibility for health administration until at least 1874. The old Bray barracks housed a voluntary dispensary (established 1812), a fever hospital (1818) and a cholera hospital (1832).[90] Only four residents were recorded in the hospital in the 1851 census[91] after which no records are found, and it appears to have closed. The major cholera epidemics struck Bray in 1832/3, 1849, 1855 and 1866,[92] slightly later than their period of occurrence in other places.

The Towns Improvement Act, adopted in 1857, gave the Commissioners some public health powers and they appointed a nuisance inspector from 1859. Yet there is little evidence of action to tackle nuisances like 'horses slaughtered every day' in the commons. And the practice of slaughtering cattle on the footpaths, a problem in 1852, may still have been continuing.[93] Indeed, as late as 1870, the Board saw no role for themselves as regards nuisances[94] and, in 1874 they 'considered that a great deal of needless expense and trouble was imposed by the [Public Health (Ireland)] Act', which spelt out their public health powers and duties.[95]

The Commissioners established a public health committee, which was technically 'the urban sanitary authority' on 5 October 1874. They concentrated on housing nuisances but also, inter alia, considered complaints related to schools, the assembly hall, car stands and a fountain, and took action against a person boiling offensive matter, against rotting seaweed and a tanning yard (in which they lost their case).[96] They concentrated on serving notices and issuing summonses, instead of abating nuisances themselves and charging those responsible – perhaps indicating reluctant compliance with statutory duties rather than enthusiasm for the task.[97]

When the 1876 Commission of Inquiry was held in Bray, there were already signs that the new thinking on public health – emphasising the targeting of individual cases – was percolating down to the town. Both the intense Dr. Whistler and the relaxed Dr. Raverty agreed that the town was surprisingly healthy despite all its public health problems, but the calculated death rate at eleven per 1,000 was considered doubtful, as Dr. Cameron had said that if true it would be 'the lowest in the United Kingdom'. Cases of typhoid and typhus were mentioned, Dr. Raverty, having seen no typhus for eighteen years and Dr. Whistler having seen one 'last year'. But the new approach to solutions was also considered. Dr. Whistler advocated a village hospital, and a 'conveyance' (ambulance) – as car men would refuse to carry patients to the hospital. He also agreed that a disinfecting chamber was needed. Limewashing of infected houses had been carried out.[98]

The 1874 Act spelt out the Commissioners powers and duties; The Public Health (Ireland) Act, 1878 codified in its 294 sections the law regulating both sanitary matters and disease control. Traditionally, local government regulated civic affairs, so no precedent was created when public health legislation, assigning uniform centrally controlled functions to local authorities, provided powers of enforcement. These were either specific powers or authority to make bye laws (for general rules) and engage in licensing and registration (permitting specific activities in specific circumstances on specific conditions). Assigning the duty of enforcing such regulations to local authorities provided a much more effective system of enforcement than had so far existed. Previously a deprived individual, living in slum conditions, would have required very considerable initiative, ability, courage and resources to challenge, by private action, a powerful landlord in a court of law, seen by the plaintiff in its setting, its culture and its personalities as an alien institution.

Bray Town Commissioners produced comprehensive public health bye-laws in 1887, covering construction of buildings and streets, closets, privies, ash pits and cesspools, scavenging, keeping animals, common lodging houses, slaughter houses and markets. Some provisions replaced previous bye-laws, no copies of which apparently remain in existence.[99] They also provided registers and licensing systems for such matters as lodging houses, and slaughter-houses.

Laws provide a framework which is perfected by implementation. While there is some evidence of low-key enforcement,[100] it appears significant as regards the commitment of the Commissioners that there are no records of a public health committee operating between 1879 (when the political upheavals started) and 1892, and there was a definite gap from 1895 until the urban district council came into existence.

Traditional concern with sanitary matters was supplemented in the early 1890s by the newer concerns, such as regulating slaughter houses, dairies and cowkeepers premises, and preparing, at the government's behest, for the anticipated cholera outbreak in 1893. The Commissioners sought temporary isolation huts, and sites on which to place them. They organised trained nurses. By 1899, removal of infectious cases to hospital, disinfecting of infected premises and isolating of their inhabitants featured in minutes of meetings. People often resisted. On one occasion, the removal of a patient by workhouse conveyance was cancelled by a woman who illegally called a car instead, saying that her landlady would not allow the workhouse van to call.[101] In March 1900, Dr. Moorhead was prosecuted by the Commissioners, on instructions from the Local Government Board, for failing to report a notifiable disease. He showed, however, that his diagnosis did not require notification.[102] This prosecution indicates the government's seriousness regarding infectious diseases, and a willingness to intervene locally if necessary.

BURIAL GROUNDS

Although Edwin Chadwick identified overcrowding of burial grounds as a serious public health risk as early as 1843,[103] the problem, despite the growing population, only hit Bray considerably later. Kilmacanogue, a traditional cemetery for Big Bray Catholics was threatened with closure due to over-crowding and water pollution in 1875. Only mass protest and establishment of a grassroots management committee secured a reprieve.[104] In 1888, St. Paul's Church of Ireland graveyard, old, urban, and overcrowded, was recommended for closing by the medical officer of health, supported by a public petition (subject to preserving personal burial rights). It was opposed by a meeting of

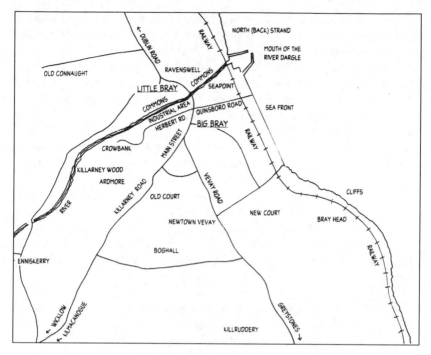

Map 4. Districts of Bray

ratepayers, mostly Catholic, who declared a new cemetery to be unnecessary. After a public enquiry, St. Paul's was declared closed.[105]

Old Connaught, to the north of the town, was the subject of criticism in November 1885. Rev. J.P. Smith wrote

> On one occasion there were two funerals going on . . . in both cases comparatively fresh remains were thrown out to make room for the new . . . a full-sized coffin lay exposed in a semi-decomposed condition.[106]

The Commissioners who, by legislative quirk, had no legal responsibility for burials until 1898,[107] complained continuously of the need since 1883 – but led the opposition themselves when a site within the town boundary was proposed, thereby truly representing the unspoken views of their constituents. The board of guardians, the authority which *had* the responsibility, tried to avoid a decision, with the establishment of committees, rejecting their recommendations, rescinding resolutions, deferring decisions, querying legal authority (following the old adage 'If you want to avoid doing anything, seek legal advice'), consulting the Local Government Board and so on.[108] They considered over a dozen different sites between 1893 and 1896 alone, bending in turn with each local pressure group or vested interest[109] and 'threw the ball back' to the Commissioners saying – will you find us a site? – only to reject the sites proposed by the Commissioners for locations outside the town. These sites had of course been previously considered and rejected by the guardians. And all the while, there was the cross-current of concern about chargeability of cost to different groups of ratepayers.[110] The anatomy of this political issue can be studied through one particular proposed site – Herbert Road at Ardmore – outside the built-up area but within the township boundary.

Here there were two vested interests, Lord Pembroke and nearby wealthy residents. They sought urgent technical advice – engineering, public health, legal. They produced their list of arguments – drainage, amenity, health, inhibition of development, devaluation of property.[111] They suggested alternatives. They lobbied the Commissioners, they held meetings, they organised deputations, they did behind the scenes lobbying ('I will see what I can do on this side of the water to crush the proposal . . . ': Lord Pembroke in London).[112] The residents called on the landowner (Lord Pembroke) to resist compulsory purchase. They used emotive terminology – 'a calamity'. They were hypocritical – 'we do not oppose a cemetery but . . . '. They secured press publicity.[113] The only typical factors in such a controversy which were apparently missing in this case, were the decrying of the 'lack of consultation' and the querying of the legality and lack of form in procedures. Maybe these would have emerged later but this proposal followed the others into oblivion.

The controversy over a new cemetery had started in November 1883 and continued beyond the end of this study. The problem was eventually 'solved' however, by the extension of St. Peter's (Catholic) and more intense use of Powerscourt (Church of Ireland) and other cemeteries.[114] In this case, vested interests twarthed for years, those promoting the more diffuse 'common good' – a not uncommon occurrence.

Yet in public health generally, a considerable improvement was achieved in Victorian Bray despite this kind of obstruction: engineering-based sanitary services were provided; sources of potential public health 'nuisances' were controlled; individual cases of infectious disease were tackled at source.

Conclusion

The rapid modernisation of Bray was to continue into the twentieth century, even though aspects of the old milieu persisted. In May 1901 when a hen lost its head in the spokes of a bicycle, the onlookers hardly dwelled on the symbolism of the interaction of old and new. But bicycles were everywhere – day trippers' cycles outside the hotel, a cycle track on the esplanade, a tricycle stolen, prosecutions for cycling on the footpath, doctors seeking exemption from this rule when responding to sick calls, cycle polo in Carlisle Grounds, the cycle shop reportedly doing very good business. And animals still held their own in town. Prosecutions for pig-keeping near houses, cases of stolen fowl, a bull at large, a mad heifer, trespassing donkeys and numerous runaway horses made the columns of the *Wicklow Newsletter*.[1]

The new technology was here to stay, however, with 'the electric light' available, cinematographic concerts in the assembly hall, a polyphone installed in the bar parlour of 'the Dublin House', an automatic vending machine at the railway station; there were telephones, motor cars and other paraphernalia of the twentieth century.[2] The urban council produced bye-laws to control road locomotives but feared that Guinness cars, which frequently frightened horses, would not be covered.[3]

Bray had changed over the previous sixty years. Off-season population was 7,424 in 1901 against 3,169 in 1841. Tourists were coming in increasing numbers, and new hotels were built around this time (the Esplanade and Lacy's). The town was providing a more sophisticated range of consumer services – from general retailing (grocers, publicans, drapers) through specialist retailers (chemists, jewellers, fancy goods, stationers, cycle engineers, pork butchers) to personal services (hairdressers, photographers, dress makers), banking and finance (two banks, Post Office Savings Bank, pawnbrokers), professional services (doctors, solicitors, insurance brokers, auctioneers), institutional services (churches, primary, secondary and private schools) as well as the public services (local government, police and courts).[4] Voluntary associations catered for a range of sporting and social activities.

What lessons can one learn from the way the community responded to the stresses of change? One could dwell on the apparent shortcomings such as the failure to develop a second Brighton, or the necessary tourist facilities – Turkish baths, floral hall or promenade pier. One could decry the sudden end to the boom of the 1860s, the loss-making harbour, or the location of the railway track. One could criticise the priorities of the civic leaders, particularly with regard to sanitary conditions and public health. However, partial success is not necessarily failure. Moreover, in common with local authorities to-day, the Town Commissioners' perceived obligations bear little relationship to the powers (mainly financial, legal and political) available to them for discharging such responsibilities.

Much was achieved – more than doubling the population in a context of a 54 per cent drop in the county population and virtually no growth in Wicklow the county town, was itself an achievement, albeit benefiting from the exodus from Dublin's inner city. The growing town was provided with the public health services it required, and it successfully adapted to the innovations of Victorian technology and thought on public health.

The legislative framework available was defective. The 'towns improvement' legislative package available was far too restrictive for a town with pretensions beyond lighting and cleansing. The alternative of private legislation was costly in time and legal expenses; so were the administrative arrangements for a response to external proposals for railways, waterworks, tramways, and other utilities affecting the township. Inter-authority disputes were often fought out expensively in court. There was a bias in favour of the ratepayer rather than the ratespender, inhibiting imaginative development proposals. In addition there was a bias for the property owner rather than the general population, resulting in a low priority being given to the needs of the poor.

The parallel between present-day politics and politics a hundred years ago is remarkable. The residents' groups, the vocational interest groups, the single issue groups all have their counterparts to-day. The politicians, despite the subsequent changes in electoral franchise, acted in much the same way as might be expected now: indeed the analogy between the search for a cemetery site in the 1890s and a travellers' halting site in the 1990s is quite remarkable.

The same political methods were also in use – meetings, deputations, petitions, lobbying – with two exceptions. There appears to be less recourse to the law in the board room now than there was previously. And the stratagem of ratepayers using the auditor, as happened so dramatically in Bray in 1874, died out, due to a number of factors, including more widely defined legal powers, political re-orientation towards need for services rather than cost limitation, changes of emphasis in auditorial practice, and the subvention of the rates burden by central government, culminating in the more recent abolition of domestic rates. However, the dampening effect of the auditorial system on creativity and innovation in the local service remained until very recent times.

Given the actual achievements noted, the imposed constraints and the further constraint of perennially trying to outmanoeuvre local vested interests, it was a creditable performance for voluntary board members who undertook this work of public service in their spare time, always subject to abuse and flak, and rarely receiving gratitude or thanks. Such is politics.

Notes

ABBREVIATIONS

B.G.	*Bray Gazette*
B.T.C.	Bray Town Commissioners records, Stores, Court House, Wicklow. Most documents have no location reference numbers.
D.B.	*Dublin Builder*
D.E.	*Daily Express*
D.G.	*Dublin Gazette*
Ev76	Evidence given to the *Royal Commission to Inquire into Local Government and Taxation of Towns in Ireland, (Report, Minutes, of Evidence, Appendices, Part I*, [*c.*1696], H.C., 1877, xxxix, 1). q. 1 = Reply to Question 1. Notes referring to the Report and Appendices of this Commission are shown in the normal form.
H.L.R.O.	House of Lords Record Office, London
H.C.C.	House of Commons Committee
F.J.	*Freeman's Journal*
I.B.	*Irish Builder*
N.U.I.M.	National University of Ireland, Maynooth
M.P.	Meath Papers, Kilruddery House, Bray
N.A.	National Archives
O.S.	Ordnance Survey
P.P.	Pembroke Estate Papers, National Archives
S.N.	*Saunder's Newsletter*
W.N.	*Wicklow Newsletter*

Note. Pagination of Parliamentary Papers refers to *printed* page numbers

INTRODUCTION

1 G.D. Scott, *The Stones of Bray* (Dublin, 1913); A.L. Doran, *Bray and Environs* (Bray, *c.*1905); 'An Old Inhabitant', *100 years of Bray and its Neighbourhood 1770–1870* (Dublin, 1907).

2 Isolde Moylan, The Development and Growth of Bray (1750–1900), (B.A. Mod. Thesis, Trinity College, Dublin, 1972); Arthur Flynn, *History of Bray* (Cork, 1986); John O'Sullivan et al. (ed.) *The Book of Bray*, (Blackrock, 1989).

3 Available in Bray Public Library.

4 W.H. Clare, 'Victorian Bray – an Administrative Perspective', M.A. Thesis 1997, N.U.I.M.; The thesis contains additional detail, maps, photographs, unabridged footnotes, bibliography etc.; copies at Maynooth College, Gilbert and Bray Libraries. Hereinafter referred to as Clare, 'Bray'.

5 O.S., 6" Dublin XXVI, 1838; O.S., 6" Wicklow IV and VIII, 1843.

6 K.M. Davies, 'Bray Co. Wicklow as a Tourist Resort, 1750–1914' in Barbara O'Connor and Michael Cronin (eds)

73

Tourism in Ireland, A Critical Analysis (Cork, 1993), pp 32–3; *Parliamentary Gazetteer of Ireland* (2 vols, London, 1846), i, p. 278.

7 Samuel Lewis, *Topographical Dictionary of Ireland*, (3 vols, London, 1837), i, pp 221–3; Davies, 'Tourist Resort', pp 31–2.

8 *Appendix. D to Sixth Annual Report of Poor Law Commissioners*, H.C., 1840, xvii, pp 206–7; *Supplement to Appendix D, First Report, Commissioners for Inquiring into Condition of Poorer Classes in Ireland*, H.C., 1836, xxxi, p. 57; *Supplement to Appendix E, ibid*, H.C., 1836, xxxii, p. 57.

9 *F.J.*, 8 Oct. 1830; *F.J.*, 24 Sept. 1831; *F.J.*, 18 Oct. 1838; *F.J.*, 16 Jan., 1843.

10 Mary Daly, *Dublin, the Deposed Capital 1860–1914* (Cork, 1985), pp 118 and 202.

THE POLITICAL ARENA

1 *D.G.*, 19 Jun. 1840; *D.G.*, 6 Oct. 1840; 9 Geo. IV, cap. 82.

2 *Minutes of Evidence, Royal Commission to Inquire into the State of Fairs and Markets in Ireland*, H.C., 1854–5, xix, p. 315.

3 See page 31

4 *F.J.*, 25 Nov. 1852; *F.J.*, 3 Oct. 1857; see page 32

5 Based, with slight amendment, on W.E.Vaughan and A.J.Fitzpatrick (ed.), *Irish Historical Statistics: Population 1821–1971*, (Dublin 1978) pp 32–3.

6 17 & 18 Vict., Cap. 103; Virginia Crossman, *Local Government in nineteenth Century Ireland* (Belfast, 1994), p. 67; 9 Geo. IV, cap. 82, and 17 & 18 Vict., cap. 103.

7 Crossman, *Local Govt.*, p. 67; *Report, Proceedings, of Select Committee on Alterations in Law relating to Local Government and Taxation of Towns in Ireland*, H.C., 1878, xvi,p. vii; Ss. 72, 77, 78 of 17 &18 Vict., cap. 103.

8 *ibid.*, Ss. 22, 25, 40.

9 *F.J.*, 9 Nov. 1857.

10 22 &23 Vict., cap. 75; see page 47.

11 *D.G.*, 18 Sept. 1857; *D.G.*, 15 Aug. 1865.

12 *Special Report to Lord Lieutenant of Ireland, in pursuance of Report of Special Committee of House of Commons July 1877, on Local Government and Taxation of Towns in Ireland*, H.C., 1878, xxiii; pp 40–41; Brian Donnelly, 'Development of Local Government in Ireland' in *Irish Archives*, iii, No. 2, (1996) p. 4; *B.G.*, 9 Dec. 1865.

13 *B.G.*, 29 Nov. 1865; *B.G.*, 9 Dec. 1865; *B.G.*, 7 Apr. 1866; *B.G.*, 16 Jun. 1866.

14 *D.G.*, 28 Nov. 1865; *B.G.*, 16 Dec.1865.

15 *B.G.*, 29 Nov. 1865; *B.G.*, 20 Jan. 1866.

16 *B.G.*, 16 Dec. 1865; *B.G.*, 13 Jan. 1866.

17 *B.G.*, 16 Dec. 1865; *B.G.*, 20 Jan. 1866; *B.G.*, 10 Feb. 1866.

18 *B.G.*, 21 Apr. 1866; *B.G.*, 25 Aug.1866; Clare, 'Bray'p. 9.

19 *B.G.*, 13 Jan. 1866.

20 Ss 13 and 31 of 29 & 30 Vict. cap. 261.

21 43 Vict., cap. 17.

22 *B.G.*, 13 Jan. 1866.

23 S. 14. of 29 & 30 Vict., cap. 261.

24 Norman Chester, *English Administrative System 1780–1870* (Oxford, 1981), pp 332, 333, 356; Ruth Hodgkinson, *Science and Public Health* (Bletchley, Bucks, 1973), p. 37.

25 Chester, *Admin. System*, pp 357–61; Derek Fraser, *Evolution of the British Welfare State* (London, 1973), p. 69.

26 Chester, *Admin. System*, pp 371–3.

27 34 & 35 Vict., cap. 109.

28 35 & 36 Vict., cap. 69.

29 H.A.Street, *The Law Relating to Local Government* (Dublin, 1955), pp 1254–7.

30 *Ibid*, 1261–5; Clare 'Bray' p. 11–12.

31 John Handcock, 'Should Local Government Acts be extended to Ireland?' in *Journal of Statistical and*

Social Inquiry Society of Ireland, v, (1869), pp 97–9.

32 *F.J.*, 6 Jun. 1874.

33 M.P., J/2/11, (5), letters Jun.1874.

34 ibid, letter 16 Jun. 1874.

35 *Minutes of Evidence, S.C. on Taxation of Towns*, pp 231–2; D.E., 16 Jun. 1874.

36 *Report Part III, Minutes etc., Royal Commission to Inquire into Boundaries and Municipal Areas of Cities and Towns in Ireland*, H.C., 1881, l, p. 248.

37 See page 13.

38 *S.N.*, 11 Jun. 1874.

39 *S.N.*, 15 Jun. 1874.

40 *S.N.*, 23 Jun. 1874.

41 *F.J.*, 18 Jan. 1875; *F.J.*,19 Jan. 1875.

42 Ev76., q. 587 et seq.

43 *F.J.*, 3 Feb. 1876; *F.J.*, 8 Feb. 1876; Ev76., q. 586; *F.J.*, 4 Apr. 1876.

44 See p. 63.

45 *F.J.*, 20 Nov. 1876; *Report, Part I, Royal Commission to inquire into Local Government and Taxation of Towns in Ireland*, H.C. 1877, xxxix, p. 19.

46 Ev76., q. 726–824.

47 Ev76., q. 298–365.

48 *F.J.*, 27 Nov. 1876.

49 Ev76., q. 837–54.

50 *Report, R. C. on Taxation of Towns*, p. 19.

51 *B.G.*, 6 Jan. 1866.

52 Ev76 q. 641 et seq.

53 *F.J.*, 16 Oct. 1878.

54 Ev76., q. 395.

55 M.P., J/2/11, (1), letters 29 Apr. 1878, 9 May 1878, 26 May 1878, 8 Jun. 1878.

56 B.T.C., Bundle 1, case stated, 25 May 1879.

57 B.T.C., Bundle 1 cases stated, 25 May 1879, 27 Jun. 1879, 10 Jul. 1879; M. P., J/2/11, (1), letter 21 Jul. 1879.

58 Reginald, 12th Earl of Meath, *Memories of the Nineteenth Century* (London, 1923), pp 133–4.

59 *F.J.*, 29 Aug. 1879; M.P., J/2/11, (2), letter 4 Dec. 1879; M. P., J/2/11, (4), letters, various dates.

60 M.P., J/2/11 (2), letter Dec. 1879; M.P., J/2/11, (6), list of costs, 30 Aug.1884.

61 M.P., J/2/11, (2), document 10 Apr. 1881, letter 13 May 1881; M.P., J/2/11, (2), letters 15 May 1881, 16 May 1881, 30 May 1881,

62 M.P., J/2/11, (4), letter 3 Mar. 1884.

63 M.P., J/2/11, (4), letter 21 Nov. 1883.

64 *F.J.*, 6 Sept. 1869; *F.J.*,11 Jun. 1872; *F.J.*, 12 Oct. 1873.

65 *F.J.*, 18 Oct.1881.

66 M.P., J/2/11, (4), letter 15 Feb. 1884.

67 *F.J.*, 27 Dec. 1883; *F.J.*, 4 Jan. 1884; *F.J.*, 7 Jan. 1884; *F.J.*, 8 Jan. 1884.

68 *F.J.*, 15 Jan. 1884; Anon. *Memories of Father Healy of Little Bray* (London, 1904).

69 *F.J.*, 14 Jan. 1884; *F.J.*, 15 Jan. 1884; *F.J.*, 22 Jan. 1884.

70 *F.J.*, 22 Jan. 1884.

71 *F.J.*, 22 Jan. 1884.

72 M.P., J/2/11, (4), letter 11 Feb. 1884; Clare 'Bray' p. 24.

73 M.P., J/2/11, (4), letters, various dates, 1882; *F.J.*, 21 Jan. 1884.

74 *F.J.*, 5 Feb. 1884; M.P., J/2/11, (4), letter 15 Feb. 1884; *F.J.*, 8 Apr. 1884; M.P., J/2/11, (5), letter 3 Apr. 1884; *F.J.*, 5 Feb. 1884; *F.J.*, 19 Feb. 1884.

75 M.P., J/2/11, (5), legal account, 26 Jun. 1883 – Apr. 1884; M.P., J/2/11, (5), letter 6 Apr. 1884,

76 *F.J.*, 14 Jan. 1884.

77 *W.N.*, 24 Oct. 1885.

78 *Report (Pt. III), etc., Boundaries Commission*, p. 243; *ibid*, pp xvi–xvii.

79 *F.J.*, 19 Jan. 1881; 44 & 45 Vict., cap. 143.

80 *W.N.*, 25 Dec. 1886; *W.N.*, 26 Feb. 1887; *W.N.*, 25 Jun. 1887; *W.N.*, 3 Mar. 1888; *W.N.*, 1 Oct. 1887.

81 *W.N.*, 25 Jun. 1887.

82 See page 40; B.T.C., copy affidavits 9 Dec. 1886, 22 Dec. 1886, 13 Jan. 1887 (two); *W.N.*, 5 Feb. 1887.

83 *W.N.* (various), 27 Nov. 1886–21 Jul. 1888; Clare 'Bray' p. 24.

84 *W.N.*, 9 Apr. 1887.
85 *W.N.*, 27 Oct. 1888; *W.N.*, 26 Oct. 1889.
86 53 & 54 Vict., cap. 161; 58 & 59 Vict., cap. 155; 59 & 60 Vict., cap. 117.
87 *W.N.*, 27 Oct. 1894; *W.N.*, 19 Oct. 1895.
88 *W.N.*, 24 Oct. 1896; *W.N.*, 24 Apr. 1897; *W.N.*, 1 May 1897; *W.N.*, 12 Jun. 1897.
89 *W.N.*, 12 Jun. 1897; N.A., Hoey and Denning presentation, box 11, mortgage 22 Nov. 1877; N.A., Landed Estates Court records, LEC 94/45, 8 Jun. 1869; *F.J.*, 30 May 1855; *F.J.*, 4 May 1882; *W.N.*, 15 Jul. 1899; *W.N.*, 7 Apr. 1900.
90 *F.J.*, 8 Nov. 1861; *F.J.*, 23 Jun. 1864; *F.J.*, 18 Nov. 1872; *F.J.*, 17 Nov. 1879; *W.N.*, 5 Sept. 1896; Clare 'Bray' p. 31.
91 *F.J.*, 25 Aug. 1884.
92 *F.J.*, 25 Aug. 1884; *W.N.*, 28 Mar. 1885.
93 *F.J.*, 23 Jun. 1864; M.P., J/2/11, (1), letter 8 Jun. 1878.
94 61 & 62 Vict., cap. 37.
95 *W.N.*, 7 Jan. 1899; *W.N.*, 21 Jan. 1889; *W.N.*, 18 Feb. 1899.
96 *W.N.*, 28 Jan. 1899.
97 *W.N.*, 26 Jan. 1901.

BUILDING UP THE NEW TOWN;
TIDYING UP THE OLD

1 Liam Clare, *Loughlinstown Workhouse in the 1840s* (Foxrock, 1986), pp 3–5.
2 9 &10 Vict., cap. 213; undated plan filed at '12–8', Engineer's Office, Iarnrod Eireann, Westland Row, Dublin, 2.
3 K.A. Murray, 'Bray Head' in *Journal of the Irish Railway Record Society*, Jun. 1980, pp 74–5.
4 *F.J.* (various), 8 Dec. 1874 to 19 Jan. 1875, and 10 Jan. 1877 to 17 Apr. 1877.
5 *F.J.* (various), 23 Feb. 1876 to 12 Jun. 1876; *F.J.*, 6 Jan. 1877; *F.J.*, 2 Feb. 1877; *F.J.*, 1 Mar. 1878; M.P., J/2/11, (5), case stated 19 Dec. 1872; P.P.,

1011/7/5, Bray Improvement Bill 1866, (annotated); Clare 'Bray' p. 36
6 *W.N.*, 3 Mar. 1894; *W.N.*, 10 Mar. 1894; *W.N.*, 24 Mar. 1894; *F.J.*, 16 Dec. 1873; *F.J.*, 6 Jan. 1874; *F.J.*, 17 Apr. 1877; *F.J.* (various), 27 Jun. 1882 to 30 Feb. 1883; *W.N.*, 1 Aug. 1885; *W.N.*, 3 Mar. 1894.
7 e.g. pages 33, 45, 58.
8 *F.J.*, 6 May 1853.
9 P.P., 1011/2/15., letter 12 Jun. 1858..
10 P.P., 1011/2/15., letter 10 Dec. 1858,
11 See page 62.
12 K.M. Davies, 'Bray' in Anngret Simms and J.H. Andrews (eds), *Irish Country Towns* (Cork, 1994) p. 131.
13 William Garner, *Bray Architectural Heritage* (Dublin, 1980); *Thoms Directory*, 1858–66; *F.J.*, 30 May 1855; *F.J.*, 4 Aug. 1860; *F.J.*, 2 Jun. 1862.
14 John O'Sullivan, 'The Quin Family of Bray', in *Book of Bray*, (Blackrock, 1989), pp 71–7.
15 N.A., Landed Estates Courts Records, LEC 94/45.
16 D.J. Hickey and J.E. Doherty, *Dictionary of Irish History since 1800* (Totowa, N.J., 1981), p. 114; unpublished paper, Dargan and Bray by T. Francis O'Reilly, copy with author.
17 See page 28–9.
18 *B.G.*, 5 May 1866; *F.J.*, 2 Jun. 1862; *F.J.*, 25 Apr. 1862.
19 Garner, *Bray*, p. 69; A. Flynn, *Famous Links with Bray* (Bray, 1985) p. 7.
20 Daly, *Dublin*, pp 118–9, p. 202.
21 Lewis, *Dict.*, i, pp 221–2; An Old Inhabitant, *100 Years*, pp 44–5.; Clare 'Bray' p. 40.
22 *F.J.*, 9 Apr. 1861; P.J. Walker, 'Brighton then and now' in *Sussex County Magazine*, (c.1954), pp 108–110; Anthony Dale, *Fashionable Brighton*, (London, 1967), pp 14–17; Clare 'Bray' p. 41.
23 John Parry, *The Coasts of Sussex – A Guide*, (Brighton, 1833), pp 97 et seq.; Clifford Musgrave, *Life in Brighton* (Rochester, 1981) p. 296.

24 F.J., 17 Jan. 1865; F.J., 10 Dec. 1862; F.J., 20 May 1864; F.J., 16 Nov. 1867.
25 Daly, *Dublin*, pp 200–201; B.G., 10 Mar. 1866; John O'Donovan, Article on Foxrock in *Evening Press*, 2 May 1979.
26 Daly, *Dublin*, pp 55–56.
27 John O'Sullivan, 'Quin Family' in *Book of Bray*, p. 77.
28 P.P., 1011/4/64, letter 8 Jun. 1896;
29 Liam Clare, Draft lecture, 'The Putland Family', to be published.
30 O. S. *Maps, 10 feet to 1 mile, Town of Bray*, 13 sheets, (Dublin, 1870).
31 Comparison of O.S. sheets, 1870 and 1911 editions with *Thom's Directory*; W.N., 18 Feb. 1899.
32 B.G., 6 Jan. 1866; Ev76, q. 461; W.N., 24 Dec. 1898.
33 Lewis, *Dict.*, i, pp 221–2.
34 An Old Inhabitant, *100 years*, p. 76.
35 Davies, 'Tourist Resort', p. 32.
36 B.G., 10 Mar. 1866; W.N., 13 Jul. 1901.
37 Davies, 'Tourist Resort', pp 30–31.
38 F.J., 10 Dec. 1862; F.J., 20 May 1864; F.J., 16 Nov. 1867.
39 F.J., 29 Apr. 1868; F.J., 24 Feb. 1875; F.J., 2 Mar. 1875, Valuation Office annotated valuation records – Bray, 1881.
40 J.J. Gaskin, *Irish Varieties* (Dalkey, 1987), p 175.
41 Valuation Office, Bray Records.
42 W.N., 4 Aug. 1900;
43 Valuation Office, Bray Records; W.N., 1 May 1897.
44 W.N., 4 Aug. 1900.
45 *Census, 1901, Part 1, Area, Population and Number of Houses, Vol. 1, Leinster, No. 12, Wicklow*, H.C., 1902, cxxiii, pp 65–77.
46 *Evidence, Boundaries Commission*, p. 241.
47 W.N., 24 Dec. 1898.
48 N.A., Census Returns, 1901, Forms A and B, Files 63, 64, and 82, 26/D.E.D., Co. Wicklow;
49 F.J., 28 Jul. 1856; F.J., 26 Sept. 1877; F.J., 21 May 1861; W.N., 19 May

1894; W.N., 25 May 1901; W.N., 16 Mar. 1901.
50 F.J., 14 Oct. 1859; *Appendix 37 to 3rd Report Part II, Royal Commission to Inquire into and report on certain Questions affecting Coast Erosion, and the Reclaimation of Tidal Lands and Afforestation*, H.C., 1911, xiv, p. 42.; D.B., 1 Nov. 1859.
51 S. 51 and 52 of 29 & 30 Vict., Cap. 261.
52 F.J., 2 Nov. 1869.
53 F.J., 23 Mar. 1868; F.J., 13 Jan. 1874; F.J., 17 Jan. 1877; F.J., 8 Dec. 1880.
54 P.F. Comber, 'Bray Sea Wall and Esplanade' in *Journal of Institute. of Civil Engineers in Ireland*, xix (1889), pp 101–8; James Walvin, *Beside the Seaside* (London, 1978), p. 50.; Comber Sea Wall, pp 101–108.
55 F.J., 28 Jul. 1856; W.N., 22 Apr. 1899; W.N., 20 May 1899; W.N., 14 Jul. 1894.
56 Isolde Moylan, 'The Development of Bray' in *Book of Bray*, p. 56.
57 F.J., 13 Sept. 1878; W.N., 4 Aug. 1900; W.N., 6 Nov. 1886; F.J., 29 Aug. 1876.
58 W.N., 24 Aug. 1889.
59 W.N., 22 Feb. 1890.
60 Walvin, *Seaside*, p. 73; F.J., 27 Mar. 1861.
61 Walvin, *Seaside*, p. 49.
62 D.G., 27 Nov. 1863.
63 F.J., 29 Jun. 1867.
64 W.N., 23 Sept. 1893.
65 W.N., 24 Oct. 1896; W.N., 27 Jan. 1900; Clare, 'Bray' p. 48.
66 O'Reilly, 'Dargan and Bray'.
67 F.J., 14 Oct. 1859.
68 F.J., 17 Jan. 1865.
69 F.J., 16 Feb. 1877; F.J., 14 Aug. 1877.
70 Walvin, *Seaside*, p. 23, pp. 69–72.
71 F.J., 10 Jun. 1884; F.J., 4 May 1857; F.J., 8 Apr. 1861.
72 B.T.C., copy Bathing Bye-Laws 1870.
73 F.J., 28 Jun. 1876; F.J., 28 Sept. 1877; W.N., 16 Sept. 1893.
74 B.T.C., uncatalogued printed document.

75 *F.J.*, 13 Jul. 1882; *F.J.*, 7 Aug. 1878;
     F.J., 11 Mar. 1879; *F.J.*, 28 Feb. 1880;
     F.J., 13 Jul. 1882; B.T.C., affidavit 13
     Jan. 1887; Clare, 'Bray' p. 49.
76 *W.N.*, 26 Sept. 1885; *W.N.*, 7 Nov.
     1885; *W.N.*, 6 Mar. 1886.
77 *F.J.*, 10 Oct. 1962; *F.J.*, 19 Oct. 1862;
     F.J., 26 May 1963; *F.J.*, 28 Aug. 1876;
     F.J., 4 May 1882.
78 *F.J.*, 4 May 1875; *W.N.*, 16 May 1883.
79 *3rd Report etc., R.C. on Erosion*, p.
     183; *ibid*, pp 42–44.
80 *Ibid.*, pp 42–4.
81 *Ibid.*, p. 185–6.
82 M.P., Box 2, B19/44/1, account Jun.
     1860, Bray Commons
     Commissioners; M.P., Box 2,
     B19/44/1, brief 20 Jul. 1863.
83 *3rd Report etc., R.C. on Erosion*, pp
     42–4; James Scannell, 'Bray's Night
     of Terror' in *Bray Historical Record*, i,
     no. 1, (1986), pp 9–18.
84 *Railway Magazine*, lxi, (1927), p. 315;
     Liam Clare, 'Exploring the Coast
     from Killiney to Bray', unpublished
     lecture, 1993.
85 *F.J.*, 3 Jul. 1883; *F.J.*, 18 Oct. 1885;
     W.N., 18 Feb. 1899.
86 Clare, 'Exploring the Coast'; Liam
     Clare, *Unionist/Nationalist Election
     Campaigns in South County Dublin,
     1883–1923* (Foxrock, 1983), p. 8;
     Clare, 'Bray' p. 53.
87 *F.J.*, 27 Mar. 1867; *F.J.*, 1 Feb. 1869;
     Preamble, 44 & 45 Vict., cap. 143;
     F.J., 2 Mar. 1880.
88 *F.J.*, 4 Dec. 1872; *3rd Report etc.,
     R.C. on Erosion*, pp 42–44.
89 Ev76, q. 407 et seq.; *F.J.*, 2 Dec. 1879.
90 Clare, 'Exploring the Coast'.
91 Lewis, *Dict.*, i, p. 222.
92 *Ibid.*, p. 222; M.P., Box 2, B/19/44/1,
     bill of evidence 7 Nov. 1863,
     pp 34–42.
93 *F.J.*, 4 Feb. 1860.
94 *3rd Report etc., R.C. on Erosion*,
     p. 183; s. 56 of 29 & 30 Vict., cap.
     261; *D.B.*, 1 Jul. 1861.

95 *F.J.*, 14 Nov. 1860; *F.J.*, 6 Oct. 1874;
     Ev76, q. 704 et seq., 716 et seq.,
     842 et seq.
96 *D.B.*, 1 Jul. 1861.
97 *D.G.*, 28 Nov. 1862, *D.G.*,27 Nov.
     1863, *D.G.*, 23 Nov. 1866; *F.J.*, 29
     Jun. 1867, *F.J.*,1 Jul. 1867.
98 S. 46, 47, and 56 of 29 & 30 Vict.,
     cap. 261; *F.J.*, 20 Oct. 1868.
99 See p. 51.
100 *F.J.*, 6 Jul. 1883; *W.N.*, 3 Mar. 1888,
     I.B., 1 Dec. 1893.
101 53 & 54 Vict., cap. 161; *I.B.*, 15 Jul.
     1891; Michael Suttle, 'Story of Bray
     Harbour' in O'Sullivan (ed.) *Book
     of Bray*, pp 99–102.
102 *Ibid.*, pp 99–102; *W.N.*, 8 May 1897.
103 *W.N.*, 4 Feb. 1899; *3rd Report etc.,
     R.C. on Erosion*, p. 184.
104 *W.N.*, 28 Oct. 1893; *W.N.*, 18 Feb.
     1899.
105 Arthur Doran, *Bray and Environs*
     (Bray, 1985) p. 20.
106 *F.J.*, 4 Oct. 1858; *3rd Report etc.,
     R.C. on Erosion*, p. 42.
107 Ev76, q. 117 et seq., q. 634, q. 489;
     F.J., 8 Nov. 1872; *F.J.*, 10 Nov. 1874.
108 *W.N.*, 22 Aug. 1891; *W.N.*, 26 Jun.
     1886.
109 *W.N.*, 23 Jul. 1892; *W.N.*, 20 Jan.
     1894; 58 & 59 Vict., cap. 155;
     59 & 60 Vict., cap. 117; *W.N.*,
     22 Feb. 1896; *W.N.*, 20 May 1899;
     W.N., 18 Aug. 1900, *W.N.*,
     22 Jun. 1901.
110 *F.J.*, 25 Jul. 1855; *F.J.*, 16 Sept. 1856.
111 S. 26, 22 & 23 of Vict., cap. 75; S. 53
     of 29 & 30 Vict., cap. 261; *F.J.*, 22
     Jan. 1873.
112 See pages 32, 42.
113 *F.J.*, 16 Mar. 1859; *F.J.*, 9 Apr. 1861.
114 *F.J.*, 26 Apr. 1861; *F.J.*, 11 Oct. 1864;
     F.J., 3 Mar. 1865; *F.J.*, 13 Nov. 1867;
     F.J., 24 May 1869.
115 *F.J.*, 11 Oct. 1864.
116 *F.J.*, 4 Dec. 1862; *W.N.*, 17 Feb. 1900;
     F.J., 8 Dec. 1876; *F.J.*, 3 Nov. 1874.
117 *F.J.*, 22 Jun. 1873; *F.J.*, 17 Jan. 1876.

118 Ev76, q. 186 et seq, q. 667 et seq.
119 *FJ.*, 22 Feb. 1880; *FJ.*, 13 Jun. 1882.
120 *W.N.*, 7 Nov. 1899.
121 *FJ.*, 1st Apr. 1859; H.L.R.O., notes re Bray Commons Inclosure Bill 1859, H.C.C., 21st Jul. 1859.
122 S. 37 of 22 & 23 Vict., cap. 75; M.P., J/2/11, (1), letter 20 May 1881; Ev76, q. 758, 851.
123 M.P., J/2/11, (3), letter 12 Mar. 1882.
124 Ev76, q. 760.
125 M.P., J/2/11, (4), letters 3 Mar. 1882 and 1 Jun. 1883.
126 M.P., Box 2, B19/44/1, copy mins. (various) Bray Commons Commissioners, bill of evidence 7 Dec. 1863.
127 *D.G.*, 23 Nov. 1858.
128 *FJ.*, 25 Feb. 1859.
129 *FJ.*, 1 Apr. 1859.
130 *FJ.*, 1 Apr. 1859; H.L.R.O., notes re Bray Commons Inclosure Bill 1859, H.C.C., 21 Jul. 1859; *FJ.*, 25 Jul. 1859; 22 & 23 Vict., cap. 75.
131 As note 126.
132 M.P., J/2/11, (2), case on behalf of William B. Orpen and John Ball Greene.
133 *Evidence, R.C. on Fairs and Markets*, p. 315.
134 Lewis, *Dict*, i, p. 222; *FJ.*, 30 Sept. 1844.
135 An Old Inhabitant, *100 years*, p. 35.
136 *Ibid.* p. 35; M.P., B/19/44/1, (2), bill of evidence, 7 Nov. 1863, pp 41 and 47,
137 *Evidence, R.C. on Fairs and Markets*, p. 316–7.
138 *FJ.*, 13 Dec. 1869; *FJ.*, 5 Oct. 1874.
139 *Evidence, Vol. 10, Royal Commission on Market Rights and Tolls*, H.C., 1890–91, xxxix, p. 221.
140 *Evidence, R.C. on Fairs and Markets*, pp 315–6; Ev76, q. 46, q. 395; *FJ.*, 10 Nov. 1874.
141 *FJ.*, 4 May 1875; Ev76, q. 51; M.P., J/2/11, (2), record, 10 Apr.1881; *FJ.*, 15 Dec. 1884.
142 *Evidence Vol. 10, R.C. on Market Rights*, pp 220–3.
143 B.T.C., Registry of Car Owners' Licences and Committee Minute Book, 10 Jan. 1862; *FJ.*, 23 Feb. 1849.
144 *Census 1901*, pp 65–7.
145 *FJ.*, 2 Jul. 1861; *FJ.*, 25 Mar. 1876; *FJ.*, 26 Jan. 1874; *W.N.*, 2 Jul. 1898; *FJ.*, 7 Apr. 1884.
146 Ev76, q. 393, 395, 491, 693; *Report Part 1, R. C. on Taxation of Towns*, pp 18–19.
147 Ev76, q. 395.
148 Ev76, q. 491.
149 *FJ.*, 5 Jul. 1878; *FJ.*, 17 Dec. 1872; *FJ.*, 3 Aug. 1880.
150 *W.N.*, 28 Nov. 1891; *FJ.*, 7 Sept. 1876.
151 M.P., Box 2, B/19/44/1, bill of evidence 7 Nov. 1863, p. 53; *FJ.*, 11 Dec. 1871.
152 *FJ.*, 17 Jul. 1871.
153 *FJ.*, 11 Dec. 1871; *FJ.*, 12 Dec. 1871; *FJ.*, 9 Dec. 1879.
154 *I.B.*, 1 Dec. 1893.
155 *FJ.*, 7 Sept. 1883; *FJ.*, 8 Oct. 1883; *FJ.*, 20 Mar. 1884.
156 *Report etc., Select Committee on Harbour Accommodation*, H.C., 1883, xiv, pp 193, 233; *FJ.*, 24 Oct. 1883.
157 *FJ.*, 21 Jan. 1884.
158 *FJ.*, 12 Jan. 1884.
159 *FJ.*, 27 Jan. 1880; *Census of Ireland, 1881, Part 1, Area, Population and Number of Houses, Vol. 1, Leinster, No. 12, County Wicklow*, H.C., 1881, xcvii., p. 1150.
160 *FJ.*, 15 Mar. 1884; *FJ.*, 15 Aug. 1884.
161 *FJ.*, 23 Aug. 1884; *FJ.*, 10 Oct. 1884; *Report of Inspectors of Irish Sea Fisheries for 1885*, H.C., 1886, xv, p. 9.
162 *Census 1901*, pp 65–77.
163 *FJ.*, 10 Oct. 1884; *FJ.*, 22 Sept. 1884.
164 H.L.R.O., File-Plans: *Bray Township Bill 1881*.
165 Various uncatalogued Counsel's opinions held by author in his 'Putland file 6'.

PUBLIC HEALTH

1 *F.J.*, 10 Oct. 1865.

2 Hodgkinson, *Science*, p. 4.

3 *Ibid.*, pp 45 and 61; Irvine Louden, 'Public Health Preventive Medicine and Professionalisation' in Andrew Weir (ed.) *Medicine in Society* (Cambridge, 1992), pp 252–3.

4 MacDonagh, *Early Victorian Government* (London, 1977), pp 99–102, and 136–142; Edwin Chadwick, *The Sanitary Condition of the Working Classes* (London, 1842).

5 MacDonagh, *Victorian Govt.*, p. 137; Fraser, *British Welfare State*, pp 68–9.

6 Louden, *Public Health*, pp 261–4.

7 *Ibid.*, p. 270.

8 John Ashton and Howard Seymour, *The New Public Health* (Milton Keynes, 1988), pp 17–21; E. le Roy Ladurie in intro. to Jean-Paul Goubert, *The Conquest of Water*, (English version by Andrew Wilson), (Princeton N.J., 1989), p. 1; Hodgkinson, *Science*, p. 60.

9 17 & 18 Vict., cap. 103; 29 & 30 Vict., cap. 90; 38 & 39 Vict., cap. 93; 41 & 42 Vict. cap. 52 ; F.B. Smith, *The People's Health 1830–1910* (London 1979) p. 199.

10 Jean-Paul Goubert, *Water*, p. 169 et seq.

11 per Seamus Ó Dunlaing, Bray U.D.C.

12 *D.B.*, 15 Nov. 1865; B.G., 23 Sept.1865.

13 M.P., Box 2, B/19/44/1, draft award of Bray Commons Commissioners 1867, Sch. 3, Pt. 2.

14 *Report etc., R.C. on Taxation in Towns*, p. 522–3; Ev76, q. 618 et seq.

15 O'Reilly, 'Dargan and Bray'; B.G. 23 Sept. 1865.

16 *B.G.*, 11 Nov. 65.

17 Waterworks Dept., Wood Quay, Dublin, 8, E.J. Bourke, memo. on water charges, Jan. 1960, (unpublished), p. 3.

18 M.P., J/2/11, (5), report Dec. 1864, town surveyor; *F.J.*, 6 Dec. 1864.

19 *F.J.*, 17 Jan. 1865.

20 S. 49, 29 & 30 Vict., cap. 261; *I.B.*, 15 Jan. 1867.

21 *F.J.*, 25 Feb. 1868; *F.J.*, 3 Mar. 1868; *F.J.*, 6 Aug. 1868; B.T.C., minutes, 25 May 1870; ibid., 6 Jun. 1870.

22 Bourke, Water charges, pp 11–12.

23 Ev76, q. 56, 287, 454, 286, 669.

24 Ev76, q. 289; *F.J.* 20 Nov. 1876; *F.J.*, 21 Nov. 1876.

25 Ev76, q. 294, 403, 393.

26 *W.N.*, 22 Jul. 1893; *W.N.*, 23 Sept. 1893.

27 Bourke, Water charges, p. 9.

28 Smith, *People's Health*, p 220; *Evidence, Select Committee to inquire into any plans for dealing with Sewage of the Metropolis and other Towns with a view to its utilisation to Agricultural Purposes*, H.C., 1864, xiv, p. 127 ; J.C. Wylie, *Wastes of Civilisation* (London, 1959), p. 52.

29 *S.C. on Sewage*, p. 127.

30 Wylie, *Wastes*, p. 50 et seq.; MacDonagh, *Victorian Govt.*, p. 139; Goubert, *Water*, pp 61–2.

31 John O'Sullivan 'Quin Family' in O'Sullivan, *Book of Bray*, p. 76; *F.J.*, 25 Apr. 1862.

32 B.T.C., document 'minutes relevant to sewers question [1866–1871]'; Jacinta Prunty, *Dublin Slums 1800–1925* (Dublin, 1997), p. 88.

33 B.T.C., document 'minutes re sewers', various dates.

34 *Ibid.*

35 *ibid.*, 8 Nov. 1869; ibid, 11 Jun. 1870.

36 *Ibid.*, 7 Sept. 1868; Ev76, q. 366 et seq.

37 Fraser, *British Welfare State*, p. 61.

38 B.T.C., 'minutes re sewers' 7 Dec. 1868, and 1 Feb. 1869; Ev76, q. 396 et seq.

39 See page 17; Ev76, q. 367 et seq.

40 Ev76, q. 150 et seq., q. 194 st seq., q. 396 et seq.

41 Ev76, q. 251 et seq., q. 523 et seq.

42 *W.N.*, 7 Mar. 1900.

43 *W.N.*, 2 Mar. 1901.

44 *D.B.*, 1 Nov. 1859.

45 *F.J.*,24 Sept. 1867; *F.J.*,11 Sept. 1869;
B.T.C., minutes, 19 Dec. 1870.

46 Ev76, q. 142, 399, 182; *Report etc.,
R.C. on Taxation of Towns*, pp 522–3.

47 Ev76, q. 295/6, 393.

48 M.P., J/2/11, (2), letter 23 Sept. 1883.

49 Henry Cairns, 'Sanitation in Little
Bray' in *Bray Historical Record*, No. 3,
1989, pp 40–42.

50 B.T.C., minutes, 'urban sanitary
authority' 1 Feb. 1894; *W.N.*, 4th
Aug. 1900; *W.N.* 2 Mar. 1901.

51 Lewis, *Dict.* i pp 221–3; O.S., Dublin,
XXVI, 1837, Wicklow, IV, 1838.

52 Richard Rodger, *Housing in Urban
Britain, 1780–1914* (Basingstoke,
1989), p. 30; M.P., Box 2, B/19/44/1,
evidence to Bray Commons
Commissioners, 21 Nov. 1859;
uncatalogued draft case 1858, in
deed box held by Misses Toler-
Aylward, Paulstown, Co. Kilkenny.

53 H.L.R.O., notes H.C.C. on *Bray
Commons Inclosure Bill 1859*, 22 Jul.
1859.

54 *Ibid.*, 21 Jul. 1959.

55 M.P., Box 2, B/19/41/1, copy minutes, Bray Commons Commissioners,
6 Dec. 1859 and 5 Jul. 1860,

56 McDonagh, *Victorian Govt.*, pp 135–7.

57 *Ibid.*, p. 156; Fraser, *British Welfare
State*, p. 69; W.H. Wickwar, *The Social
Services* (London, 1936), p. 107.

58 MacDonagh, *Victorian Govt.*, p. 157.

59 See page 33.

60 *F.J.*, 14 May 1859; Ev76, q. 244.

61 B.T.C., board minutes, 10 Oct. 1870.

62 B.T.C., minutes, urban sanitary
authority, 5 Oct. 1874–14 Jul. 1879.

63 *Ibid.*, 1875 and 1876, various dates;
Ev76, q. 215; *F.J.*, 10 Aug. 1875; *F.J.*,
20 Mar. 1876; *F.J.*, 20 Nov. 1876.

64 B.T.C., minutes, urban sanitary
authority, (1874–1878); Ev76, q. 254
et seq.

65 *F.J.*, 7 Nov. 1876.

66 Ev76, q. 164.

67 Ev76, q. 196 et seq.

68 Ev76, q. 205 et seq., 237 et seq., 284
et seq.

69 Ev76, q. 201 et seq., 212 et seq., 237
et seq., 257 et seq., 221 et seq.

70 Ev76, q. 154, 231, 256, 561; B.T.C.,
minutes 'urban sanitary authority', 5
Oct. 1874, 27 Nov. 1874, Jan., Feb.,
Mar. 1875.

71 *F.J.*, 21 Nov. 1876; Ev76, q. 426 et seq.

72 Ev76, q. 449, 587, 610, 475; *Report etc.,
R.C. on Taxation of Towns*, pp 522–3.

73 *F.J.*, 13 Dec. 1876.

74 M.P., J/2/11, (1), letter 26th May
1878.

75 *F.J.*, 28 Apr. 1879; *W.N.*, 28 Jul. 1894;
W.N., 2 May 1891; Ev76, q. 72, 395.

76 Sir Charles Cameron 'On clearance
of unhealthy areas', in *Dublin Journal
of Medical Science*, lxxxiii, (1887), pp
326–33.

77 B.T.C., minutes, 'urban sanitary
authority', 12 Oct. 1899, *W.N.*, 17
Mar. 1900.

78 *F.J.*, 15 Dec. 1874.

79 M.P., J/2/11, (4), letter 17th Mar.
1883; M.P., J/2/11 (3), report 4 Jun.
1883; M.P., J/2/11, (2), letter 20 Oct.
1887; M.P., J/2/11, (5), letter 30 Dec.
1953; *3rd Report etc., Royal Commission
for inquiring into the Housing of the
Working Classes*, H.C., 1884/85,
xxxi, p. 96; *F.J.*, 14 Aug. 1877.

80 Daly, *Dublin*, p. 298; Smith, *People's
Health*, p. 226.

81 *R.C. on Housing*, p. xi.

82 Cameron, Clearance of unhealthy
areas, p. 326–33; 53 & 54 Vict., cap. 70.

83 *F.J.*, 25 Nov. 1884.

84 *W.N.*, 3 Feb. 1900; *W.N.*, 17 Mar.
1900; 63 & 64 Vict., cap. 192.

85 Rodger, *Housing, Britain*, p. 31;
George Vanston, *Law Relating to
Public Health in Ireland* (Dublin,
1892), p. 5 – quoting *Glen's Public
Health*, 10th ed., p. 135.

86 W.H. Clare, Statistical Analysis of
Census Material relating to
Victorian Bray, unpublished.

87 F.J., 30 Nov. 1867; B.T.C., Minutes urban sanitary authority, 11 Sept. 1876; F.J., 14 Nov. 1876.
88 Ev76, q. 229, 263, 441; *Report etc., R.C. on Taxation of Towns*, pp 522–3.
89 B.T.C., minutes 'urban sanitary authority', 30 Mar. 1893; *W.N.*, 26 Jun. 1900; *W.N.*, 17 Mar. 1900.
90 *Appendix B to First Report, R.C. on Poorer Classes*, H.C., 1835, xxxii, pp 285–7.
91 *Census of Ireland, 1851, Part 1 (area, population. and number of houses), Vol. 1, Leinster, County Wicklow*, H.C., 1852–3, xci, p. 355.
92 As note 90; Clare, *Loughlinstown Workhouse*, p. 22; F.J., 5 Jan. 1855; F.J., 10 Oct. 1866–5 Dec. 1866.
93 F.J., 14 May 1859; H.L.R.O., Evidence 21 Jul. 1859, H.C.C. on *Bray Commons Inclosure Bill; Report of R.C. on Fairs and Markets*. p. 317.
94 See page 62.
95 F.J., 6 Oct. 1874.
96 B.T.C., minutes 'urban sanitary authority', 5 Oct. 1874 to 8 Dec. 1879; F.J., 12 Dec. 1876; F.J., 13 Sept. 1878; F.J., 29 Aug.1881.
97 Ev76, q. 162.
98 Ev76, q. 261, 537, 550, 594, 551, 283, 266, 267, 277, 281.
99 *Byelaws, Bray Township*, (Dublin, 1887).
100 *W.N.*, 2 May 1891.
101 B.T.C., minutes 'urban sanitary authority', 17 Nov. 1892 to 2 May 1895 and 11 May 1899 to 12 Oct. 1899; *W.N.*, 22 Oct. 1898.
102 *W.N.*, 3 Mar. 1900; *W.N.*, 10 Mar. 1900.

103 Fraser, *Welfare State* p. 59; Henry Jephson, *The Sanitary History of London* (London, 1907), p. 36.
104 F.J., 22 Feb. 1875; F.J., 11 May 1875; F.J., 17 Sept. 1875.
105 *W.N.*, 26 Nov. 1887; *W.N.*, 10 Dec. 1887; *W.N.*, 28 Jan. 1888; *W.N.*, 18 Feb. 1888; N.A., Local Government Board, Order No. 121/1888, 30 Apr. 1888.
106 *W.N.*, 6 Mar. 1897.
107 S. 160, 41 & 42 Vict.,cap. 52, amended by S.29, 61 & 62 Vict., cap. 37.
108 *W.N.*, 27 Jun. 1896; *W.N.*, 19 Oct. 1895; *W.N.*, 15 Aug. 1896; *W.N.*, 17 Nov.1894.
109 *W.N.*, 22 Jul. 1893 to 29 Aug. 1896.
110 *W.N.*, 4 Jul. 1896; *W.N.*, 15 Aug. 1896; *W.N.*, 12 Aug. 1893.
111 P.P.,1011/4/64, report 25 Jul. 1896.
112 P.P., 1011/4/64, letter 8 Jun. 1896.
113 P.P.,1011/4/64 (various documents); *W.N.*, 27 Jun. 1896; *W.N.*, 13 Jun. 1896.
114 *W.N.*, 6 Mar. 1897.

CONCLUSION

1 *W.N.*, various dates, mainly 1900–1901.
2 *W.N.*, various dates, mainly 1901.
3 *W.N.*, 22 Sept. 1900; *W.N.*, 27 Oct. 1900.
4 *Thom's Directory 1901*; N.A., Census Returns 1901 – Co.Wicklow, 26/D.E.D., 5, 34, 43, 63, 64; 27/D.E.D. 9.